"Most people have a dread of confrontation. This is partly because most people do it very badly. I often give my clients information about good confrontation. Now I don't need to, because it is all here. Good stuff and worth pursuing!"

Dr John Rowan, author of *Ordinary Ecstasy*

"In a style that is warm, engaging and encouraging, this book invites us to enrich our conversational lives. We are shown that our conversations are pivotal to our personal unfolding, and that we can readily learn to have 'big conversations' more skilfully. One of the great qualities of the book is that you feel as if you are having an inspiring conversation with the author."

Graham Lee, author of *Leadership Coaching*

"This book will inspire and enable you to have a big conversation, be it in your personal or business life. It is packed with practical guidance, exercises and stories that bring to life the power of skilful conversation. Sarah's critical reflection on her own story, as well as those of the people she has coached, is truly compelling. A really good read."

Dominic Mahony, Director of Lane4 Consultancy

"The best thing I've read on conversations (and how they change your life) in 20 years. Full of head, heart, hand and soul. It's practical, rigorous, deeply personal, clever and accessible. Every story connected and resonated with my life as a parent, son, husband, consultant, tutor and sometime free/unfree spirit."

John Higgins, research associate at Ashridge Business School and author of *Images of Authority, Organisational Consulting* and *Organisational Consulting*

"This is a most valuable and timely book; in today's complex world it is increasingly important to engage authentically with people who matter to us. Sarah helps us through practical tools and personal stories to discover how pivotal conversations can help us to mature and grow."

Dr James Pritchard, learning consultant, Civil Service Learning

"There are a very few moments that we recall as truly significant shifts in our lives. These often if not always come through conversation. Read this book and understand why – a powerful guide to genuine growth and change."

William Isaacs, author of *Dialogue and the Art of Thinking Together* and Senior Lecturer at MIT Sloan School of Management

"We evolve through conversation. When you are willing to change the conversation you are having, with others or with yourself, it can literally change your life. This great book shows you how."

Robert Holden PhD, author of *Shift Happens!* and *Happiness NOW*

"Conversation is key to enhancing our relationships. This book gives you powerful tools so you can have heart-to-heart interactions that will be make your relationships more rich, fulfilling and transformative."

Marci Shimoff, *New York Times* bestselling author of *Love for No Reason* and *Happy for No Reason*, and featured teacher in *The Secret*

"*Life-changing Conversations* by Sarah Rozenthuler is the epitome of excellence in the art of introspective communication. This powerful book provides the tools, tactics and strategies to enter a world of Big Conversations with others and ourselves. These conversations become the trajectories for a much deeper insight into ourselves and the world around us. If getting the most out of life is important to you, you must read *Life-changing Conversations!*"

Eldon Taylor PhD, FAPA, radio personality and *New York Times* bestselling author of *Choices and Illusions* and *Mind Programming*

"*Life-changing Conversations* is a vital, useful, practical book which will assist you in learning how to share your own personal truth with others. This book delivers precisely what the title states. And I highly recommend it!"

Christiane Northrup, MD, ob/gyn physician and author of the New York Times bestsellers *Women's Bodies, Women's Wisdom* and *The Wisdom of Menopause*

"*Life-changing Conversations* is a gem – insightful, thought-provoking, well-written and based on good psychological theory and practice. For decades psychologists and therapists have known the value of simply talking, yet people still underestimate the power of conversations. In this book the author provides an expert and compelling insight into conversation, ably and seamlessly linking theory to practice, making the complex easily accessible and inspiring readers. I thoroughly recommend this book to anyone interested in learning more about the power of conversations."

Neil Anderson PhD, Professor of Human Resource Management and Director of Research at Brunel Business School

"This book needed to be written. Succinctly and by means of intriguing stories, it gives us hints and skills that can save a marriage, broker a deal or start a magnificent future – for someone, and quite conceivably for you. Sarah Rozenthuler has insights into the ways we need to talk with each other to make sense of the challenging years that lie ahead of us. She has the inside story on how we need to connect, in order to evolve as a species."

Dr Scilla Elworthy, Nobel Peace Prize nominee and founder of the Oxford Research Group and Peace Direct

Sarah Rozenthuler is an author, spiritual educator and leadership development consultant, with over 10 years' experience working with large organizations such as the World Bank, the BBC, BP and the UK Civil Service. She specializes in the field of "dialogue", helping business leaders and their teams to have more creative, powerful conversations about what matters most.

Sarah has co-facilitated several retreats with Neale Donald Walsch, best-selling author of *Conversations with God*, who has called Sarah, "The next best thing to me." She has led cutting-edge mind-body-spirit events since 2007, which have earned her an international reputation.

Sarah has a first class degree in psychology from the University of Nottingham, and a post-graduate certificate in spiritual development from the University of Surrey. However, her real masterclass in handling people and group facilitation was four years working as a street circus performer, juggling fire in the *fiestas* of Spain.

Life-Changing Conversations

7 strategies for talking about what matters most

SARAH ROZENTHULER

WATKINS PUBLISHING
LONDON

This edition first published in the UK and USA 2012 by
Watkins Publishing, Sixth Floor, Castle House,
75–76 Wells Street, London W1T 3QH

Design and typography copyright © Watkins Publishing 2012

Text copyright © Sarah Rozenthuler 2012

Diagrams on pages 170, 174, 201, 237, 251, 256 and 263 copyright
© Sarah Rozenthuler 2012

1 3 5 7 9 10 8 6 4 2

Design and typesetting by Jerry Goldie Graphic Design

Printed and bound in China

British Library Cataloguing-in-Publication Data Available

Library of Congress Cataloging-in-Publication Data Available

ISBN: 978-1-78028-110-0

www.watkinspublishing.co.uk

Distributed in the USA and Canada by Sterling Publishing Co., Inc.
387 Park Avenue South, New York, NY 10016-8810

For information about custom editions, special sales, premium and
corporate purchases, please contact Sterling Special Sales
Department at 800-805-5489 or specialsales@sterlingpub.com

For Mum and Dad,

with thanks for all our conversations –

the big and the small

CONTENTS

PART III – THE KNOW-HOW

FOREWORD

Throughout my life I have always felt – and experienced – that there is no problem between people who love each other that cannot be resolved by talking about it. The power of conversation is enormous. Yet I can tell you that in 25 years of spiritual coaching with over 10,000 people, I have actually encountered (more than I ever suspected that I might) an enormous reluctance on the part of even those in normally close, loving relationships to exchange, in direct conversation, information about "what is so" for them.

The plain fact is that many people are simply loathe to enter into open discussion about anything they believe could be the least bit self-revealing – to say nothing about minimally unpleasant or mildly confrontational. I wondered about this for some time, because I know that at our core most of us yearn to be *known* and to be *heard*. How could these two attitudes exist side by side in such a huge swath of humanity?

Then I began to see the problem. The issue was not that people did not want to be revealed, nor that they had no tolerance for the exploration of even gentle differences. The issue was that many people simply felt ill-equipped to have such conversations. They didn't have confidence in their ability to "hold their own", or to "keep cool", or to avoid eruptive emotions or to stay away from accusatory or blaming or hurtful language.

The result is that many people find themselves continuing in an unpleasant or unwelcome or unworkable situation in order to avoid the unpleasantness of talking about it. So they endure one unpleasantness to avoid another.

Yet now comes Sarah Rozenthuler to tell us that conversations or exchanges that "clear the air" do not have to be unpleasant, and can actually create more pleasantness than ever before in all manner of situations – even situations that we want to bring to an end.

Life-changing Conversations throws a lifeline to those who are drowning in silence, living moments (and sometimes entire lives!) of "quiet desperation". Here are techniques, approaches and verbal devices that work – in short, the tools that most people wish they had when they wish things were different.

Sarah reminds us that compassion, caring, patience, understanding and love can find their way into our most difficult conversations. Indeed, can form the *basis* of them.

In life, there are conversations and there are *conversations*. And therein lies the trick. How to use conversation to produce desirable outcomes is what we all want to know more about. A wonderful spiritual teacher once advised me: "Speak your truth, but soothe your words with peace." In nine words, this is what the remarkable book you are now reading is all about.

If you have a little difficulty in expressing your feelings or confronting your own truth, this could be one of the most important books you've ever come across.

Thank you, Sarah, for this extraordinary contribution.

Neale Donald Walsch

Part I

The Foundation

Introduction

If you could have a conversation that would change your life, who would it be with? Your partner, a colleague, your boss, a neighbour? And if you found a way to talk, what difference would your Big Conversation make? Would it help to clear the air, heal a hurt or renew a relationship?

I believe that conversation is pivotal in our lives, yet many of us are holding back from talking. We fear upsetting other people, losing our job or damaging the love we have. This book gives you the know-how to have that conversation, leave your baggage behind and move forward in your life.

By enhancing our ability to talk together we can create the lives that we desire, for ourselves and for those whose lives we touch. If one of us finds the courage to talk, then another does, then another, this domino effect could even change the world.

We are living in times of great change – technologically, socially and financially. Many of us are experiencing upheavals that we never could have anticipated even a short while ago. Whether we have to step into a new arena of work, draw a line under a relationship or uproot from our home, we have to roll with the punches as never before.

In the midst of this turmoil, the need for heart-to-heart, human-to-human encounters is becoming ever more pressing. As we hurtle toward a future full of unknowns, many of us feel increasingly disorientated. With tomorrow's technology arriving before we've even mastered today's, we can feel isolated behind our computer screens, haunted by the conversations we're not having.

Navigating these uncharted waters calls for a new set of capacities. We need an expanded sense of self, new skills and bridge-building tools to reconnect with each other. Whatever the form of the particular challenge we face — a broken relationship, an unexpected situation at home or a significant career choice — we can equip ourselves to ride these shockwaves of change. We can learn to have life-changing conversations.

The ability to discover new ways of relating to one another is of paramount importance. Many of us are facing tough times and difficult decisions. We might want to speak out about something that matters, release ourselves from an out-dated commitment or create a more meaningful life. Common to many of these challenges is one element: interacting with others. When another person is involved, a further factor comes into play: having a conversation.

* * *

A skinny 17 year old

I remember well the first time a conversation changed the course of my life for ever. I was a skinny 17 year old, taking my A-level exams. I'd spent the previous four years agonizing over which degree I was going to take – a decision that my parents had told me would affect the rest of my life. I had an offer from the University of Nottingham to read architecture, a subject that I'd selected at the tender age of 13. I'd chosen my A-level subjects in maths and science to support this decision, even though I was more of an artistic type at heart.

The evening before my final exam, the dinner conversation took an unexpected turn. It was the late 1980s and, in the small town of Shrewsbury where I'd been brought up, close to the Welsh border, families still ate supper together. My mum looked at me across the table and said:

"I don't think you really want to study architecture, do you?"

I was astounded. I thought I'd known for years what I wanted to be when I grew up.

"What makes you say that?" I asked, slowly.

"Well," Mum continued carefully, "Whenever I bring up the subject of you going to Nottingham, you don't want to talk about it. I know you'll enjoy university, so the only thing I can put it down to is that you don't want to study architecture."

"I, err …"

I was lost for words. I left the dinner table and went upstairs to my room. Closing my algebra books, I put away all my revision notes and sat at my desk staring out of the window. As my breathing slowed down, I could feel my shoulders drop and my whole being relax. I thought about how being an architect had really been my dad's dream. I admitted to myself how hopeless I was at three-dimensional geometry, how hard I found technical drawing and how much more interested I was in people than in floor plans. I was no more an architect than I was an engineer, my dad's chosen profession, which lacked the creative outlet he needed.

As I sat there, poised on the edge of my adult life, I felt the truth of my mum's words pulsing inside me. She had voiced something I'd known but hadn't known that I'd known. I felt a huge sense of relief as I realized that I didn't want to become an architect after all. As I watched the sun slip below the skyline, little did I know that, as a result of a short talk with my mum, my life would fork down a different path entirely.

* * *

That conversation proved to be a turning point. Without it, I'd never have switched to studying psychology, specialized in organizational psychology or become a dialogue consultant. I wouldn't have written this book, you wouldn't be reading it and there would probably be a few more quirky buildings in some corner of the world.

Although the conversation seemed to come out of nowhere at the time, years later I learned that, for my mother, it had been a different story. After many discussions with my father about whether to say anything to me or not, she'd weighed it up, turned the conversation over in her mind and come down on the side of needing to speak out. She'd then chosen her moment, found the right words and given me the space to absorb their impact. My mother is a maestro of life-changing conversations.

Expanding our capacity to talk, particularly when we face critical choices, is a life-enhancing skill. I believe that there is no faster way for us to evolve than through the process of interacting with one another. Our relationships — in our personal, professional and intimate lives — are the ultimate arenas of growth. We come to know who we are and what we're about by talking with one another.

A conversation at a crossroads in our life offers us a huge opportunity to take a leap in our own evolution. Even more importantly, it perhaps enables us to make a contribution to the wider development of humanity at this volatile and unpredictable time. Today, many hope for a global society where each person's needs are met, but this is a dream we will only bring into being if we can talk to each other and listen.

Why I have written this book

My hope for this book is that it will change your life. I intend that it will inspire, equip and stir you to have your own Big Conversations. By reading it may you open your soul to new depths, lift your life to new heights and mend the part of the world that is yours to tend. After reading these pages, I trust that you will be able to talk with anyone, anytime, anywhere, and discuss what matters most without running scared or getting shy.

To create a world in which we can all live well together, we need to become more conscious participants in our conversations. In my experience, Big Conversations don't just happen. We must prepare for them, stretch into them and be present to them. It is all too easy to overlook the power of conversation. It is such a mundane, humble tool that we take it for granted. If we want conversation to change our lives, we need to play our part and do our work to integrate our outer and inner worlds.

Outwardly, there are communication skills we can practise, tools we can use and attitudes we can adopt. These give us the flexibility we'll need when we reach out to someone else to talk. It is often not easy to "go over to the other side" and meet another person in dialogue, while staying true to ourselves. Having some action guidelines increases our confidence and competence in doing this.

Even more important, however, is the inner work that a Big Conversation necessitates. The wider perspective, the more generous spirit, the calling forth of our best energies — all these flow from a deepened sense of who we are. Any significant change in our outer reality, including our conversations, is always preceded by a shift in our consciousness. True dialogue is, in its best moments, technique-less.

This book is, therefore, a tapestry, woven from various threads. It has emerged out of hundreds of coaching sessions and thousands of conversations - with family and friends, colleagues and clients as well as pioneers in "dialogue". I've also knitted in some of my own experiences with Big Conversations.

The book draws together tools from the field of dialogue, insights from the discipline of psychology and wisdom from the "new spirituality". This potent mix can transform how we talk together and how we act in the world and our lives.

How to use this book

In **Part I**, I describe how conversation is the main medium through which our lives unfold and how making small changes can make a big difference. I outline what undermines a conversation and explain how becoming more conscious, creative participants helps to change how we talk for the better.

In **Part II**, I describe the Seven Shifts in consciousness that enable us to have life-changing conversations. I explain them through the stories of seven people who have "gone to their edges" to find a way to talk at critical moments in their lives, from leaving a relationship to taking on a new job.

In **Part III**, I offer some exercises to help you to have Big Conversations of your own. When we know how to prepare, talking together – even about the tough stuff – is easier than we imagine. It is not necessary to do all the exercises; completing one may be enough to create the shift that's needed. Use your intuition and go where your energy flows.

The Seven Shifts

The heart of this book is what I have called the Seven Shifts. These will enable you to have life-changing conversations. The shifts are to:

- **Call up your courage** – to right a wrong, be bold and talk about what's been pushed under the table.
- **Create a container** – to renew a relationship, heal a hurt and talk about what's been lost and forgotten.
- **Intend the message you send** – to stretch into the future, break out of a stuck situation and talk about what you really want to do with your life.
- **Connect with respect** – to make life more meaningful, voice your deepest desires and talk about what matters most in a way that honours the other person.

- **Speak your truth** – to set yourself free to live the life you choose, say the "hard truths" and talk without compromising who you are.
- **Surrender your story** – to stop playing small and to become conscious of how you might sabotage the conversation, so you can talk about new possibilities.
- **Find closure** – to restore your peace of mind, free up your energy and make the conversation the start of a new beginning.

The tales in this book are of ordinary people living their everyday lives. This is a deliberate choice. While I've spent more than 10 years working as a consultant psychologist to large organizations such as the UK Civil Service, the World Bank and the BBC, it's been the one-on-one conversations in the kitchen and in the bedroom, more than in the boardroom, that have been most instructive.

Not everyone is a senior executive, business leader or civil servant. However, many of us are mums and dads, partners and lovers, brothers and sisters, friends and neighbours. Seeing how other people have changed their lives through changing their conversations will, I hope, arouse you to see new possibilities for yourself.

Each of the seven stories is based on a real-life person or persons, with all identifying details changed. I have created composites where necessary to protect identities. I am deeply grateful to those who chose me to accompany them when they'd reached an impasse in their interactions and needed to find a way to talk. Helping each of them to prepare for, build up to and absorb the impact of their Big Conversation has been an honour and an education.

I believe that when we deepen our awareness, the ordinary becomes extraordinary and an everyday encounter can become a life-changing conversation. When minds meet, hearts open and souls touch, talking together gives us glimpses of a larger reality. We remember who we are, how we are unique and what we came here to do.

With seven billion of us now on this planet, there are some big things that need to be done for us to live together in harmony. The good news is that big things are achieved through the small steps that we each can take. Having a life-changing conversation is one of them.

CHAPTER 1

Small changes make a big difference

In this chapter we're going to explore:

- Why conversation matters
- What conversation is – and isn't
- The question "Can we talk?"
- How conversational skills can be learned
- How life unfolds through conversation
- How small changes make a big difference

Why conversation matters

Conversation is centre stage in most people's lives. We might even see the whole of life as one conversation followed by another and then another. Talking together is what many of us spend a large portion of our time doing, whether it's across the kitchen table, in the office or at a party. Making changes to how we talk can, therefore, have a big impact on our lives.

I became interested in conversation at a young age. As I listened to grown-ups talk, I discovered some patterns that years later have informed my practice as a dialogue coach. Even more valuable to me, however, was the realization of how much our everyday lives revolve around conversation. Before I share with you what I noticed, let me tell you the story of how I became such a keen observer of conversations.

* * *

I was 10 years old, exhausted and ill. I'd been studying night and day, preparing to take the entrance exam to senior school a year early as my mother was a teacher and keen to accelerate my education. The doctor told my parents that I should stay at home for several weeks to recover and, as Mum was working, my grandmother stepped in to look after me.

I was curious to find out exactly how Min (as my grandmother is known to family and friends) spent her time. She was retired, having worked for more than 25 years as a receptionist at a local rubber factory. Always active, highly social and fond of pottering around in her garden, Min liked to be busy.

I soon got to know the rhythm of her days. Most of our time was spent visiting Min's friends in a never-ending round of coffee mornings. I could never figure out whether these women had husbands or not, but none were ever present. Perched on my chair at the side of the room, drinking orange squash out of a plastic beaker, I watched how the women interacted. When I was with my friends we'd play and run about, whereas what these grown-ups did was *talk*.

To stop myself getting bored, I invented my own games. My favourite was to see if I could recall the thread of the women's conversation. I'd make a note in my head of the first subject someone talked about and then try to follow the different topics: recipes for homemade raspberry jam, then supermarkets, the new library and so on, until the conversation ended with Mrs Jones's hip and Uncle Fred's funeral.

To my frustration, I found that I often couldn't keep up with the flow of the conversation. It seemed to meander all over the place. It was tricky to follow the women as they gossiped, swapped recipes and whispered their secrets to one another. The conversation swirled in unexpected directions, circled back on itself and found new courses to follow.

Something else also struck me. While Min and her friends would often begin with an apparently unimportant subject, like making chutney, the talk would gradually move on to more meaningful territory, such as family, health and loss. As each of them spoke in turn and the conversation flowed, it would naturally drop into a deeper place.

Many coffee mornings later, I came to appreciate that talking together was the glue that kept these women connected. It was how they supported each other, shared their stories and found solace in their often solitary lives. Conversation was what kept them *alive*.

* * *

Listening to my grandmother and her friends talk made me realize that even an apparently trivial conversation brings great benefits. Talking together:

- Forms friendships
- Brings comfort
- Airs issues
- Informs our decisions
- Creates new ideas
- Deepens connections
- Changes how we think about things

No wonder we spend so much of our time talking! The research bears this out. If I asked you what proportion of your waking life is spent talking to other people, what would you say? When I put this question to managers and leaders at the dialogue workshops I run in the corporate world, the typical response I receive is somewhere between 40 and 80 percent. Moreover, a consistent pattern emerges: the more senior a leader, the more time he or she spends interacting with others.

A survey carried out in 2010 by Courage Beer also reveals how much we talk in our everyday lives. They found that in a sample of 3,000 British adults, the typical person has 27 conversations a day, lasting an average of 10 minutes each. This adds up to a rather staggering 4½ hours a day talking.

Even more revealing, however, was the finding that while conversations were very commonplace, nearly half of them (43 percent) were deemed to be pointless. If we were to make our conversations more meaningful, it would make a huge difference to the quality of our lives. And this brings us to the question of what makes a good conversation.

What conversation is – and isn't

Not every verbal interaction is a conversation. A shouting match is not a conversation. A debate in parliament is not a conversation. A presentation with a short question-and-answer session tacked on at the end is not a conversation. Two people talking over each other and not listening is not a conversation.

Coming from the Latin *con* meaning "with" and *versare* meaning "to turn", the essence of a conversation is "turning together". The rhythm of a good conversation is not prescribed, like a cha-cha-cha or two-step, but an improvisation in which each person moves in response to the other. We don't know where it will go, no one is in control … but on with the dance!

Building on my coffee-morning experiences, here are a few observations I've made about what makes an exchange of words a conversation:

- Everyone who's present participates.
- Each person says what's true for them.
- Everyone is listened to.
- People talk about what really matters.
- No one tries to control where the conversation goes.
- People respect each other's differences.

A real conversation opens up new possibilities. By talking with one another, we can arrive at an answer we never anticipated, resolve a situation that's got stuck and decide on a new direction. As thoughts spark across the space between us and catch light, we feel our lives rekindling.

That said, conversation is not a silver bullet that can solve all our problems. Sometimes we have to swing into action without further discussion. Other times we need to hunker down and wait until the storms of change blow over. In times of not talking, however, it is wise to ask ourselves whether turning away is the right thing to do or the only thing we're able to do. There's a big difference, as we shall see.

Can we talk?

At many of the critical points in our lives, such as deciding whom to marry, what organization to work for or whether to have children, the essential question is, "Can we talk?" Often used as an invitation to talk, "Can we talk?" can be a way of signalling that something of significance needs to be said.

However, the question "Can we talk?" has another side to it. It also means, "Are we *able* to talk? Can we continue the conversation without one of us sliding into a silence or into verbal violence?" Our inability to stay in the room and talk together is the root cause of many problems between husbands and wives, parents and children, and diplomats from different nations.

Many of our verbal interactions fall short of being a real conversation. We stay polite, not saying what's really going on.

When we aren't listened to, we withdraw or, like the British tourist abroad, we speak louder in the hope that this time we'll be understood. There are many ways in which a potential conversation can crash.

The good news, however, is that we can learn to talk together more effectively. Having a life-changing conversation is within reach of all of us. As with other forms of art, the key is to practise in the right way. Having some know-how enhances our ability to engage others. Let me share with you how I learned this.

* * *

After graduating from university with my degree in psychology, my boyfriend and I headed off to Spain in an old campervan. I had abandoned an offer to do a PhD, deciding that sunshine, siestas and sangria were more me. My plan to support myself by teaching English started to go awry, however, when our van was broken into and most of my possessions were stolen. I couldn't find a job and my savings dwindled. I started hanging out in the streets of Valencia, meeting musicians, artisans and circus performers.

While my university certificates were hard earned, they couldn't, unfortunately, feed me. My new companions, on the other hand, were all able to busk and earn their living through music, mime or making handicrafts. I was particularly envious of Jan, a 14-year-old New Age traveller from Germany, who was a master at throwing and catching a diabolo on a short string between two sticks. As I was soon to be without a peseta in my purse, I followed his example and set about learning to juggle.

With some dedicated practice, it wasn't long before I could keep a cascade of balls going without too many drops. I started "doing time", as it was called by buskers, by going pat-pat-pat at the side of a busy street when the locals took their evening stroll. After a couple of hours I'd have about a thousand pesetas (roughly £5) in coins, which at that time was enough for a trip to the supermarket.

Some months later, when the Mediterranean heat had got too much, we decided to head north to the Basque Country and try our luck at San Fermin. This is the *fiesta* where at least one American tourist dies each year running through the streets of Pamplona with the bulls.

One afternoon, as I walked through the main plaza, I noticed a fellow busker, El Mago ("The Magician"), carefully picking his pitch. I watched as he surveyed the street, laid down his bag and unpacked his props. Over the next 15 minutes he gathered a huge crowd, entertained them with tricks, such as linking ropes and removing bras from the female members of his audience, and finally collected fistfuls of paper money in his well-worn top hat. Here, I thought, is a true magician.

It turned out this savvy, street-wise 55-year-old from New York had worked his way around the world several times, financed by the takings in his hat. In exchange for lifts in our campervan between cities, I asked El Mago to coach me on how to up my game and make my fortune.

The first thing he said to me was, "You don't want to be doing time, you want to be doing shows!"

Over the next few months, El Mago taught me how to build a crowd, keep them entertained and then extract money from them. I found out how much more fun it was to make people laugh, clap and cheer together, than to stand alone at the side of the street juggling. Getting people involved also made a huge difference to the amount of money that landed in my hat. I earned the same amount in a show of 15 minutes as I had in two hours "doing time".

The real turning point came when my magician coach shared with me his top tip for a successful show: "Get a volunteer and you'll double the money in your hat!"

El Mago showed me how to select someone who'd be game and make them the centre of the show. I learned to ask them for their name and to get the crowd to give them a round of applause. When I rolled out a mat and asked Pedro, Paco or Pablo to lie down, anything could happen. Some took to the ground without a second thought, others hesitated and at least one chap walked away.

When I got out my juggling knives, it was even more uncertain what would happen next. One of my victims might laugh, another might cup his hands over his vulnerable bits and another might heckle. The finale of the show was El Camino de la Muerte – the Road of Death. I'd juggle over the top of my volunteer, from feet to head, knives flashing in the dark to the roar of the crowd.

Just as El Mago had forecast, I did indeed double the money in my hat – and more. By bringing in a volunteer, I had made the show unpredictable, spontaneous and participative. I had to improvise, use my wits and deal with whatever arose in the moment. Compared with "doing time" at the side of the street, I was now earning 20 times as much. My monologue had turned into a dialogue. I had struck gold.

* * *

On my return to the formal workplace several years later, I started to relate what I'd learned on the street about engaging others to what I was discovering about dialogue.

When I became a consultant psychologist, I was brought into many different organizations and government agencies to work with diverse people and teams across a whole range of settings. I began to notice how a project would stand or fall as a result of how well people worked together, which was a reflection of how well they talked together.

Among team members there were often disputes over strategy, debates on implementation and disagreements about resource allocation. Strong relationships could withstand the pressure of these difficult conversations. Where the relationships between people were fragile, the challenging conversations were either avoided or created further antagonism.

I was keen to help the teams that were falling apart to have the robust conversations they needed. To guide my interventions, I reflected on what I'd learned about human-to-human interactions:

- When we make our encounters more interactive, we feel more energized.
- When we allow space to improvise rather than work from a script, the conversation comes alive.
- When people feel supported and respected, they are more likely to step into the unknown.
- When we gather our energies together, we can achieve results way beyond anything we can do on our own.

Making like a good psychologist, I decided to discover if there was any research to support my observations in the field. Despite my best attempts to escape the rigours of a scientific education, I had been trained to ask, "What's the evidence?" So, with my eyes now fixed on the empirical horizon, I set off to see what I could find out about conversation from the experts.

Conversational skills can be learned

To my delight I soon came across a compelling piece of research carried out by Marcial Losada and Emily Heaphy, published in the *American Behavioural Scientist* (February, 2004). These researchers observed the conversations of 60 management teams, each of about eight members, in a large information-processing organization. Their dialogue was recorded, analyzed and evaluated across three key dimensions, explained below.

The researchers found that high-performing teams did indeed talk together in ways that were distinct from low-performing teams. In the teams associated with greatest profitability, best customer satisfaction and highest evaluations by colleagues, the team members had developed the capacity to talk with each other in some clearly observable ways.

I took a closer look at how conversational skills were making a difference to the teams at the top. These team members had developed three capabilities:

1. They asked questions as often as they asserted their own opinions (a 1:1 ratio between enquiry and advocacy).

2. They showed as much interest in others as they did in themselves, rather than being stuck in self-absorption (a 1:1 ratio between focus on self and on others).

3. They made many more positive than negative comments, so that enthusiasm, encouragement and support far outweighed sarcasm, criticism or cynicism (3:1 ratio of positivity to negativity with 6:1 as the ideal).

When all three of these behaviours were demonstrated, they created an "expansive emotional space" in which the team interacted. The atmosphere was buoyant, trusting and resilient. By contrast, in low-performing teams where people did not feel connected with each other, the atmosphere was cynical, distrustful and tense. The teams that could talk together were the most profitable and were rated most favourably by their customers. They had found their way to double the money in their hat.

When I reviewed this research, one thing became very clear: these capabilities for having productive, performance-enhancing conversations could be learned. What's more, these were key skills not only for senior executives and corporate teams, but for *everyone*. Feeling inspired, I asked myself what I else I might be able to learn about dialogue. The answer was, "A great deal".

Life unfolds through conversation

I found out about "dialogue" as a field of practice through a conversation at a workshop on complexity theory. I was keen to learn more about the science of "complex systems" having been introduced to it during my final year at university. The head of the psychology department had jettisoned his curriculum of 25 years on applied psychology to teach us about this new approach to science. When there was an uproar among the students, he responded, "This is so much more exciting and useful. Besides which, you're students, be radical!"

This cutting-edge thinking had emerged out of the conversations between scientists from different disciplines, such as biologists, economists and meteorologists. By talking together, they'd come to realize that the complex systems they studied— which could be an ant colony, the stock market or a weather front—shared some important characteristics. For one thing, their long-term future was essentially unknowable. Even the most powerful computer cannot forecast whether it will rain or shine at a specific place in the distant future with any degree of reliability (a pattern which appears not only during British summertime!).

As I read some of the first books and papers being published by scientists at the Santa Fe Institute in the early 1990s, I felt a stirring of excitement deep inside. I learned that a further characteristic of complex systems is that they sometimes operate at the "edge of chaos". This is defined as a special region where there is enough stability that a system can survive and yet also a certain degree of creative disorder, so that the system is vibrantly alive. It is in this zone of "bounded instability" that a system's evolution accelerates. For this reason, ambiguity, accidents and synchronicity are to be embraced as they can propel a complex system to re-invent itself in extraordinary and unpredictable ways. Here, I thought, is science grappling with life in the real world.

It turned out that my professor was right, not only about the scientific revolution that the complexity approach was to spark, but about its usefulness. In Spain, when I struggled with the messiness of life on the road, I often found myself going back to what I'd learned about uncertainty as a catalyst for accelerated evolution. As my own life teetered on the proverbial edge of chaos, I took comfort from the fact that this is where the true evolution of complex systems occurred. When I framed the fluidity of my life (which felt like a complex system to me) as the perfect environment for learning, I could embrace the experience instead of heading back to England defeated.

Because complexity theory had helped me to stay steady amid so much flux, when I returned to more conventional life four years later, I was keen to find out how the thinking had developed. In the UK, a think tank at the London School of Economics was applying the ideas beyond the natural sciences to organizational dynamics and attracting an eclectic mix of people from all over the world. At one of their workshops, when I shared with another participant that I was working in the civil service, I had what turned out to be yet another pivotal conversation in my life.

"If you like complexity theory and you're a psychologist," he said, "take a look at the emerging field of 'dialogue'. It's all about how interactions between people can create new and unexpected futures."

Before *we* take a closer look at dialogue, let me share with you another story. This time it's about a conversation I had as a direct result of my explorations of this leading-edge thinking about human interaction.

*   *   *

It took me over a year after leaving Spain and arriving back in the UK to summon up the strength to go job hunting. While I knew that my years travelling had provided some of my richest and most vibrant experiences, I doubted that a future employer would see it that way. I resisted writing my CV for many months as I struggled to find the words to fill the large space under "Career history".

I eventually found a job working for the Department of Work and Pensions in Sheffield. Feeling as though I had to make up for lost time, I decided to buckle down and work my way toward becoming a chartered organizational psychologist. I felt this would give me some credibility to balance the perception that I'd run away with the circus.

After three years of hard slog designing fair and open recruitment systems for civil servants, I decided it was time for the next adventure. I was keen to move south not only to progress my own career, but also to support my husband who was (and is) a tango and jazz singer. He'd left his native Buenos Aires to be with me and I knew that South Yorkshire was only going to contain him for so long. London called.

Every few months, I would catch the early morning train from Sheffield and head to the Cabinet Office just off Trafalgar Square. I was a regular at the quarterly meetings of a cross-government recruitment network. At one of these gatherings I found out that the Cabinet Office wanted to implement a radical redesign of its Fast Stream graduate recruitment programme. This is one of the longest-standing selection systems in the world and a legend among organizational psychologists.

I plotted my next move carefully. I worked out whom I needed to talk to, what I wanted to ask and when to make my approach. I'd learned from the Santa Fe scientists about the importance of interactions and how these were particularly sensitive to "initial conditions". A tiny change in the behaviour of a system early on can, over time, lead to dramatically different outcomes further down the line.

As intended, at the end of the next meeting, I waited as the head of the Fast Stream programme said his goodbyes. I could hear my heart beating like a drum in my chest and my mouth was so dry that it hurt when I swallowed. As he started to gather his papers, I went up to him and took a deep breath. I was determined to infuse our interaction with the behaviour of the bold.

"Michael," I said, "Have you got a couple of minutes to talk?"

"Sure," he replied.

I gulped, giving away my nerves. "The changes you want to make to the Fast Stream selection process sound very exciting. What are your timescales?"

"We've got about a year to finish," he replied. "We've just recruited a Principal Psychologist who joins us next month so we can get started."

"It sounds like there's a lot of work to do." I was on a roll now. "I wonder if you need any more psychologist resources? We have a new scheme in my department to set up secondments. I'd love to come and work at the Cabinet Office for a few months. Would you be interested in discussing this further?"

*   *   *

I may never have succeeded in calling up my courage for the conversation with Michael if I'd not had a sense that our interaction might catapult me into a completely new future. By that time I'd also read the seminal text by Bill Isaacs, *Dialogue and the Art of*

Thinking Together (1999). Here, another piece of the puzzle of how we can change our lives through conversation fell into place.

In Bill's book I was excited to find both a theory of dialogue and some models of practice to bring the theory alive. It was a lengthy and enlightening read, but one idea in particular stood out for me. This was the principle of "unfolding", as conceived by David Bohm, the quantum physicist with whom Bill had worked over many years.

According to Bohm, everything we see in our world arises from and returns to an invisible reality, which he called the "implicate order". This rather obscure idea came alive for me when Bill shared a powerful image of Bohm's. Typically, Bohm said, when we plant an acorn and it grows into an oak tree, we think of the seed as the source of the tree. It is, however, more accurate to see the total environment as giving rise to the tree – the moisture in the air, the nutrients in the soil and the energy from the sun. "The seed is the *aperture* through which the tree unfolds," Bill wrote (my italics).

Aperture. The word fired my imagination and ignited all sorts of questions in my mind. What if, I said to myself, I was to see each conversation as an opening through which my life unfolded? What difference would it make to my life if I engaged with another person in a way that kept the space between us as expansive as possible? How might I cultivate conversations that are apertures through which new life flows?

Inspired by Bill's work and David Bohm's ideas, I started to pay much more attention to the conversations I was having. Seeing them as openings that allowed me to glimpse a larger reality made me more aware of my everyday interactions. When I realized that just one conversation could open or shut the door on a whole new future – for me and for those around me – I felt urged to become more *conscious* of how I talked with other people.

Returning to the story of my interaction with Michael, it turned out that he *was* interested to talk more. A few months later my husband and I were happily re-creating ourselves as Londoners. Our lives had turned onto a different track entirely as a result of that short talk. I was starting to appreciate how something as simple as a conversation is a powerful way to create change in our lives.

How small changes make a big difference

One of the great benefits of creating change through conversation is that it is something we can do for ourselves. We don't need anyone else's permission or approval. We don't need a budget or a mandate. What's even more encouraging is that making even a small change to a conversation can have a far-reaching impact.

Scientists are increasingly aware of how one tiny event can change everything. Complexity theorists have eloquently described how, in a world where everything is connected, a small change over here can cause a big change over there. Over time a system's behaviour can take a radically different path as a result of an almost undetectable occurrence early on. A flap of a butterfly's wings in Beijing can change the course of a hurricane in Haiti a week later. This pattern of a slight difference making a large impact also applies to our conversations.

* * *

A few years ago I was asked to facilitate the away day of a large team in a central government department. There were around 30 civil servants of different grades, from senior managers to administrative assistants. Their leader was keen to have them all involved in a conversation so they could generate a shared vision for the future. In order to find out what was really "top of mind" for the rest of the team, I spent some time talking with several individuals in the run up to the meeting itself. Through these more informal conversations it became clear to me that, as well as coming up with a new vision, the team also needed to air their anxiety over possible job cuts, a topic that was not formally up for discussion.

In the morning, after an initial welcome, we spent some time "checking in", with each person sharing something about how they were feeling and what was on their mind. In smaller groups they then discussed what was unique about their work as a team and what they had in common with the rest of the department.

Toward the end of the morning, we came back together in a large circle for a whole-group conversation. When one of the team asked if this was going to be a group therapy session, I reassured him that it wasn't, nor would there be a group hug at the end. I had learned to expect a whole range of reactions to sitting in a circle for a conversation. Some people find this a rather radical and unsettling departure from the usual set-up of the leader being at the front of the room "talking at" the rest of the room sat in rows.

After letting the team talk for a while, I intervened. I'd been asked to give some input on dialogue and felt it was the right moment to say a few words. I explained a few key concepts about what makes a productive conversation, including the wider perspective that can be brought by a "bystander" who makes an observation about the conversation.

To help the group to ground this in their own experience, I asked if there had been any examples of perceptive bystander observations in the whole-group conversation that we'd just been having. We agreed that there hadn't.

"Would anyone be willing to make an observation now?" I asked.

There was a pause. A few seconds later, one of the longer-standing members of the team started speaking in a quiet voice.

"We've just had the same conversation that we've had at every single away day for the last seven years," he said.

I felt a ripple of agreement move across the room. To begin with no one said anything, but I could see heads nodding and people sitting up in their chairs.

As it was nearly time for lunch, we agreed to continue the conversation in the afternoon. Over lunch I suggested to the team leader that we abandon our agenda for the rest of the day, so that we could allow space for people to talk about what *really* needed to be discussed.

* * *

A small change can make a big difference to a conversation. A simple observation can refocus a discussion that's going off track. A smile can keep someone talking instead of closing down. A laugh can crack the static that's built up in the room. A touch on the shoulder can bring comfort when there are no words to say.

In the meeting of the civil servants, one simple observation led to a completely different conversation after lunch. In the atmosphere of authenticity that was activated by that one bold observation, the team could go on to voice their concerns about the threat of job cuts and what this would mean for them individually and collectively. Out of the "realness" of this conversation, a vision for the team emerged easily and effortlessly and they committed to having more conversations as a whole team.

Thus I came to appreciate, early in my explorations of dialogue, the value of the small.

While I was working at the Cabinet Office, I started training with some of the pioneers in the field of dialogue. I got in touch with Peter Garrett, who had worked closely with Bill Isaacs and David Bohm. I'd heard that he was a master at facilitating conversations, particularly among large groups, and I was keen to learn more.

We started our three-day programme with 20 of us sitting in a circle without any tables. Each person said who they were, where they were from and what had drawn them to the programme. As the "check-in" unfolded, it felt as though the room was swelling with the richness of human experience and the joy of finding connection with each other.

In between the more formal teaching sessions, we had time for agenda-free dialogues. I was struck by how easily the conversation flowed. Compared with the stilted and stale meetings I was used to back in the Civil Service, I found myself on fire with the creative ideas and insights that were emerging in the group. Not since the coffee mornings of my youth had a conversation in a group setting felt so alive.

On the final morning of the programme, I awoke early. It was still dark. I sat bolt upright in bed, feeling energy surge up my spine. "This is what I want to do," I said to myself in the hush of the dawn. It made so much more sense to me to communicate in this way, where each person's voice was valued, new thinking could emerge and lives could be changed.

A year later, when Peter Garrett offered me a full-time job, I decided to follow my dream and become a fully fledged dialogue consultant. For the next few years, I participated in and facilitated conversations among groups of different sizes, from two to 200 people. I sat in circles talking with trade union reps in oil refineries, inmates in maximum-security prisons and senior leaders in luxury hotels. Whether it was coming up with a new strategy, getting teams to break out of their "silos" or rebuilding broken relationships, dialogue was the key. Yet the good news is that it takes only little adjustments to make this happen. Whether the conversation is taking place in a boardroom or the bedroom, there are small changes we can make to how we talk together that can turn a conversation into a life-enhancing encounter:

- Let each person say something at the start about how they are or what's on their mind (known in dialogue as a "check-in").
- Listen and build on what someone else has said so that the conversation has a flow.
- Say when there is a disagreement, clearly and respectfully, so that this can be dealt with in the room rather than aired outside where nothing can be done.
- Share an observation about how the conversation is going, particularly if it's going off-track or needs refocusing.

These are the little hinges on which big doors swing open …

CHAPTER 2

It's not what we say, but *how* we say it

In this chapter we're going to explore:

- How technology is changing the way we communicate.
- Why it helps to understand that conversations can be challenging.
- What are the behaviours that kill a conversation.
- Why it's not what we say, but *how* we say it that matters.
- How our beliefs deaden dialogue.

Conversation is what makes us feel connected with each other. If you think back to the beginning of a close friendship, how did it all start? What happened when you first met? Often it began by talking together. Good conversation can create a lifelong friendship, a happy and harmonious family life and a successful business partnership.

In our increasingly computerized world, quality conversation is becoming scarcer. Many of us find it easier to text, tweet or email than to talk. Technology is changing the way we communicate and while it means that we can more easily be in contact, it doesn't always mean that we're in touch, soul to soul.

Raising our awareness about what makes conversation challenging does not remove the difficulties. It may, however, make us more receptive to dealing with them and less likely to sabotage the conversation when we do reach out. Understanding what undermines a conversation — our behaviours, our beliefs and the energy we transmit — will enable us to engage more effectively with one another.

There are moments in all our lives when a person-to-person conversation is called for. When there are important things to say and we turn and walk away, it can end a relationship for ever.

How technology is changing the way we communicate

When I was growing up in the 1970s, we had no mobile phones. We'd go out and play all day and our parents wouldn't worry about where we were. When I started working in the early 1990s, there were no laptops. Bosses dictated letters to secretaries who took notes in shorthand and used typewriters.

These days we hide behind computer screens and send emails to colleagues who sit next to us. Away from our desks, we keep constantly connected through our smartphones. We can have multiple interactions going on at the same time – and none of them a real conversation. In this age of digital connectedness, many of us feel disconnected.

Electronic communication is not all bad news. Tools such as email and texts are convenient, efficient and quick. Here are some of the things they can be great for:

- Arranging meetings
- Asking for information
- Telling someone what's happening

- Sharing a joke
- Letting someone know you're thinking about them
- Sending a message without interrupting someone.

At work, electronic communication enables us to keep an "email trail", a record of an exchange to which we can refer. In our social lives we can share photos and links to YouTube videos and keep up-to-date with our friends via Facebook.

There are, however, several significant drawbacks to this "lean communication", as it is sometimes called. These disadvantages become increasingly problematic when we need to talk about something that we care deeply about:

- **It's harder to build trust**. With electronic communication, we don't have the social cues that our species relies on to decode messages — the flickers across the face, the look in the eyes, the placing of the body. If we do not speak with someone, we miss the resonance of their tone of voice.
- **People are less likely to be honest**. When we can hide behind an email or a text, it becomes more tempting to lie. Because we do not actually have to face the recipient when we send an email, we might feel that we can get away with lying or withholding information that we would otherwise feel we have to share.
- **It's easier to disengage**. Because the communication happens at a distance, we can disconnect more easily. While this can have its advantages, it can also stop a deeper communication from developing. If we feel that the other person might log off at any point, we are less likely to open up.
- **Misunderstandings are more likely**. Because there's usually a delay between a message being sent and a reply being received, it's harder to create a flow in

the communication. By the time we read someone's response it may have become irrelevant, as we're in a different frame of mind to the one we were in when we pressed the send button.

As human beings, we miss face-to-face communication when we don't have it. We try to compensate by using what's available to us — adding "emoticons" (emotion faces) to our texts, writing in capitals in our emails or using coloured text to emphasize our words. Yet no smiley face can replace the warmth of a hug, no "LOL" can substitute for having a laugh together and no ☹ can convey how sorry we feel when there's sad news. There are times we just need to talk.

Why it helps to understand that conversations can be challenging

Even before the explosion of social media, many of us avoided face-to-face conversations. Why? Talking is such a simple activity. How difficult can it be? In my own life, I've sometimes waited years before saying something to someone. Not days, not weeks, not months but *years*. Yet the desire to communicate would not go away. It was only when I couldn't live my life of quiet desperation any longer that I finally reached out to the other person and said, "Can we talk?".

In my coaching, I've seen client after client agonize over whether to have a conversation. Careers have languished, marriages have dwindled and friendships have withered all because of our inability to talk.

Conversation is at the heart of how we relate to one another. It charges our relationships with strength and vitality. The French author Andre Maurois called a happy marriage "a long conversation that always seems too short". Heroines in Jane Austen's novels often enquired about potential suitors by asking, "Is he a man of conversation?" If he wasn't, he was not favourably regarded.

Science confirms that conversation can make us happier. Recent research reported in *Psychological Science* in 2010 found that a happy life is one filled with reflective, substantive conversation and not just small talk. Psychologists found that greater well-being was related to spending less time alone and more time talking to others: The happiest participants spent 70 percent more time talking than the unhappiest participants. Moreover, the happiest participants had twice as many meaningful conversations as the unhappiest participants. These findings suggest that to have a happy life and feel good, we need to have substantial conversations rather than having superficial ones or being solitary.

Before she married Brad Pitt, Angelina Jolie divorced fellow actor Billy Bob Thornton. In an interview for *The Sunday Times* magazine (18 July 2010), Angelina describes how the day came when they looked at each other and realized they had nothing to talk about anymore. Game over.

So what is it that makes conversation so challenging? I believe there's a clue in the following definition of conversation, which I've adapted from *The Devil's Dictionary* by Ambrose Bierce: "A fair for the display of the minor mental commodities, where each exhibitor is too intent on the arrangement of his own wares to observe those of his neighbour."

Several factors make conversation a tricky business. If we understand these, we can be more forgiving of ourselves and of others for not talking. We might even see a way through some of these challenges:

- **Engaging with someone else**. We have to listen to the other person and be receptive, rather than staying in the space of "on my terms".
- **Letting go of control**. We have to respond in the

moment to what the other says, rather than having everything worked out in advance.

- **Opening ourselves up.** We have to make ourselves vulnerable by sharing what we really think and feel, rather than hiding behind a mask.

Conversation can therefore feel risky, unpredictable and uncontrollable. When there are "meaty" things to discuss, no wonder talking can feel like such a stretch.

Accepting that we can't bend the other person to our will, that we have to give up some control and that we must take a chance to open up are big shifts. However, when we can say "yes to mess", we can have that Big Conversation and change our life.

The behaviours that kill a conversation

When was the last time you withdrew from someone? What made you back off? Was it something they said or something they didn't say? We often draw a line under a relationship because of poor communication. Conversation gone wrong can leave us feeling depressed, angry and disappointed.

There are three main clusters of behaviour that undermine a conversation. It's my observation that, under pressure, we each have a tendency to demonstrate one of them. None of the behaviours is any worse than the others — each is problematic in its own way. Conversation becomes difficult when we:

- **Fight** – attack or blame the other person by spewing out our words.
- **Take flight** – withdraw or shut down by swallowing our words.
- **Freeze** – seize up or go rigid because of not being able to access our words.

It is, perhaps, easiest to see how fighting can wreck a conversation. When you "blow your top", it can be difficult to find a way to repair the damage afterwards. A friendship that's taken years to build up can be destroyed within minutes. While a short burst of anger can be a healthy discharge of energy, shouting that lasts for more than a few seconds runs the risk of ruining a relationship.

However, flight can be just as hurtful. When someone refuses to talk, it can leave us recoiling in pain. One friend spent years trying to "process" a relationship that had been cut off without a conversation. He'd talk and talk and talk with me about it because he wasn't able to find completion with the woman who'd turned her back on him. By being denied a conversation that may have taken minutes, his heart was scarred for years.

When we freeze in a conversation, our brain shuts down and we stop talking. Our eyes glaze over and our body tenses up. We can no longer think straight or feel what's going on inside. We lose our connection with ourselves and with the other person. When we unplug, there is no conversation.

It's not what we say, but *how* we say it that matters

We see a man with a grey beard sitting on a flattened cardboard box on the street. Many people walk past, ignoring him. A few coins are dropped in his tin next to a sign that reads:

I'm blind
Please help.

Along comes an obviously well-heeled woman who pauses, picks up his sign, scribbles something on it and props it back up again. As she walks away, we hear the clink of coins being dropped, followed by more clinks, then more. The coins keep rolling in. A while later, when the same woman returns, the man recognizes her footsteps and asks,

"What did you do with my sign?"

She bends down, touches him on the shoulder and says, "I wrote the same, in different words".

The changed sign says:

It's a beautiful day and I can't see it.

This short film, "Change your words, change your world", has had, at the time of writing, more than seven million viewers on YouTube. Created by online content specialists Purple Feather, its popularity reflects the power of the message it intends to send: it's not so much what we say as *how* we say it that matters.

The importance of how we communicate is supported by scientific research. Professor John Gottman, an academic psychologist at the University of Washington, is able to predict with 95 percent accuracy whether a couple will still be married 15 years later, based on an hour's film of how they talk together about a contentious issue. When spouses show defensiveness, criticism, stonewalling or contempt, it could well involve a costly trip to the divorce court.

I learned about the difference that *tone* makes to a conversation some years ago when I worked as a dialogue consultant to an oil refinery. The threat of industrial action hanging in the air, the operations manager asked a colleague and me for help with talking to the trade union reps, who were objecting to a decision by the managers to reinstate a supervisory role. The two sides had tried to discuss the decision but ended up withdrawing to their corners, each accusing the other of unpicking previous agreements. The management team saw the union reps as disruptive and difficult; the union reps saw the managers as disrespectful and incompetent.

A three-day negotiation meeting was approaching and the risk of further fracture was high. If the negotiations were unsuccessful, strike action would be likely. This could close the refinery and cost the business millions of dollars. Reaching an agreement at the negotiation was critical.

In the run up to the meeting, my colleague and I talked with both sides, separately. We wanted to listen to everyone's concerns so we could start to create a more conducive atmosphere in which they could talk together. To meet with the operators represented by the trade union, we put on hard hats, blue overalls and huge steel-toecap boots. We drove to various tin huts around the site where the crews talked to us about their grievances over a mug of tea. After checking us out and deciding we were safe to talk to, they told us their issues and joked about getting us new boots.

On the first day of the negotiation, we were taken to a windowless room in the middle of the refinery. The managers and union reps filed in and sat down on opposite sides of the large, rectangular table. The atmosphere was tense. My mouth was dry and my head hurt. A thick wad of papers in front of me detailed job descriptions, union procedures and management policy. I braced myself for a long three days.

Before my colleague could open the meeting, a trade union official, the Chairman of the Safety Committee, stood up and cleared his throat. Silence swept across the room. Holding a sheet of paper in his hand, he started to read out the statement he'd written about a former colleague. "It is a year since Tom was enjoying some friendly banter at the start of a shift, when suddenly his life changed for ever …."

He described a serious accident that had nearly killed an operator for whom he'd issued a permit to work. Although all the correct procedures had been followed, the union official still asked himself whether he could have done anything different, whether one more site visit would have prevented the accident. This was not a speech about making further changes to the refinery's operations. It was a plea from the heart to take health and safety seriously and to remember a man who had lost his health and his livelihood due to an accident.

When he sat down, the room was completely silent. My colleague and I sat still. The operations manager quietly thanked him for honouring the anniversary and for the reminder of what really mattered. She read out the agenda a little more softly than I'd been expecting and laid out the ground-rules a little less stiffly. When the next union rep started talking, she listened carefully and paused before responding.

The negotiation lasted the full three days. Each side made its "killer points" and called for time-out when the tension got too much. During these recesses, my colleague and I encouraged both sides to keep on listening to each other. At the very last hour, they reached an agreement about the role of the supervisor. They'd been able to find a way to talk with each other. There had been respect in the room from the start.

More than anything we say or do, it is how we *are* that matters when we talk together. When we show warmth rather than talk down to someone, it keeps a conversation flowing. Being respectful instead of distant makes the other person more likely to engage. Giving some appreciation, rather than dealing out criticism, keeps the door to dialogue open. The tone of a conversation is the axis on which it spins.

How our beliefs deaden dialogue

Why is it that our differences so often lead to conflict? According to David Bohm, we need to look further "upstream" from how we're talking to how we're *thinking*. The boundaries between nations, Bohm was fond of saying, have been created entirely by human thought. In my busking days, when we drove across the Pyrenees from France into Spain there was no physical change in the landscape and the people were pretty much the same. While their language, customs and habits might be different, these are all a product of thinking. Had there not been an official at border control waving us on, I would never have known I was crossing from one country to another.

Human thought undoubtedly brings great gifts. It has structured our world, from our buildings and our possessions to our philosophies and today's ever-changing technology. It can also, however, do great harm by creating divisions between us. With so many conflicts in the world involving nation fighting nation, we forget where these false boundaries come from. We see our differences as real things rather than as ideas we've created. As a result, we feel distant from one another and find it hard to talk.

It is our *thought* that creates the boundaries between us. However, we don't realize this. Thought has structured our world, from our buildings and our possessions to our philosophies and today's ever-changing technology, but it can do great harm. It can create divisions between us. We see our differences as real things rather than as ideas we've created. As a result, we feel distant from one another and find it hard to talk.

Through my coaching work, I've found that there are seven thought patterns in particular that cause barriers to a conversation. For each of these inhibitors, there is a shift in consciousness that will transform it. I will describe these shifts in detail in Part II. For now, here are the seven inhibiting beliefs that kill a conversation:

Inhibitor 1 – "I can't talk about it"

"I'm really scared to talk with Thomas," Mary confesses. "He's a dying man and I want to be compassionate, but I also want to ensure that I don't lose what I'm entitled to. How can I find the courage to have the biggest conversation of my life?"

For many of us, a Big Conversation triggers anxiety. We don't know how the other person will respond, how talking will impact our relationship and how our life will change as a result. Our fear of the unknown can, if we let it, override our ability to step out of our comfort zone and into a conversation.

It is fear that makes us close down and cling to the status quo. Even thinking about the conversation makes adrenaline pump around our body. We feel sick and we're so afraid of feeling like this, we turn away from talking. The conversation goes on hold and so does our *life*.

Inhibitor 2 – "I don't know how to reach out"

"I've walked away from all our other encounters feeling despondent," Lily reflects. "I desperately want to connect with my dad but I don't know how to reach out. I want to explore whether our relationship can be healed before it's too late."

When we feel heavy-hearted, it can stem from a belief that we're unable to connect with someone. We can tell ourselves that we're too different, they're too remote and that the gulf between us has become too wide to bridge. Not wanting to make ourselves feel more vulnerable, we shut down.

If our relationship is in tatters, we can become trapped by the terror that a conversation will make matters worse. We crave the connection but resist reaching out. Thinking that we don't have the resources to handle the conversation, we turn away from talking.

Inhibitor 3 – "I can't decide what to do"

"I know I'm being 'wishy-washy' by not saying anything,"
Pete admits, "I just don't know what to say. I've been
married for nearly 20 years and I can't decide what to
do. I want to make a change, but I don't know how to
go about it."

We can become paralyzed by the prospect of having a conversation. As we're not clear exactly what to say, we tell ourselves it's better not to say anything. The churning inside continues and we carry on feeling stuck.

When we believe that we don't know what we want, it creates tension inside. This spills out of us and others pick up on our restlessness. We send out mixed messages: we're not happy where we are, but we're not doing anything about it. Conversation is difficult when there's a state of confusion about whether to talk.

Inhibitor 4 – "I don't want to hurt their feelings"

"My heart isn't in staying anymore," Vida discloses.
"I want to talk with Alex but I don't want to hurt his
feelings. How can I talk with him in a way that sets me
free to be me yet still honours him and my family?"

Being afraid to hurt another person's feelings is an enormous barrier to having a conversation. Sometimes our truth changes and we think that we'll betray someone if we voice how we now feel. We say nothing rather than risk damaging a relationship.

While we might think that we're being sensitive to the other person, we're really being controlled by fear. It is our fear of being rejected that makes us not want to go against someone else. We can convince ourselves that we're looking out for their feelings, when in fact we're hiding from our own. Talking together then becomes a near-impossible task.

Inhibitor 5 – "I don't know what to say"

"The conversation with my boss, Alison, is on my mind all the time," Tim divulges. "I feel like a real wimp, but I don't know what to say. How can I speak my truth without damaging the relationship? I don't want to burn my bridges at work."

When we don't know what to say, it's sometimes because we think our truth is too uncomfortable to hear. We're afraid of the backlash if we speak out. Sensing that we might be judged and found unworthy, we go silent.

Truth telling often brings discomfort. To avoid this, we make certain subjects off limits. Once something becomes "undiscussable", it's hard to make a change. To let ourselves off the hook, we tell ourselves that we simply can't find the words and we avoid the conversation.

Inhibitor 6 – "I'm right, you're wrong"

"I feel I'm being completely undermined," Teresa says. "I can't believe it, but I think I'm being bullied again. Jim's out to get me. He's behaving appallingly."

Many of us like to think that we're right and everyone else is wrong. It's one of the most seductive feelings we can have. We're sometimes willing to end a relationship, walk out of a job or damage our health all because we want to feel that we're *right*.

A mind-set of "victims and villains" is a great inhibitor to conversation. It makes us rigid and unreceptive. It leads the other person to resist what we say, as nobody likes to be shown to be wrong. When minds close, it's difficult to talk.

Inhibitor 7 – "It's too hard to talk about it"

"It feels like a big crash waiting to happen," Carlos declares. *"I need to have a conversation with my brother to resolve this conflict. How can I say what's been festering for months but still keep the family together?"*

The mind-set that a conversation is too difficult is a big blocker. When we think that there's a battle ahead, we stiffen up and the atmosphere becomes taut.

When we fear that a conversation will become a confrontation, we might convince ourselves that it's futile to talk. It won't change anything, we say. We've tried it before and it was a waste of time. This belief stops a conversation in its tracks.

*   *   *

Finding a way to talk is not only possible but essential. For when it comes to the "tough stuff", conversation is the only game in town.

CHAPTER 3

Introducing the Seven Shifts

In this chapter we're going to explore:

- How conversation changes when we become more conscious.
- Where the Seven Shifts come from.
- How conversation is all about S.E.X.
- How the living of our own life is the source of our wisdom.

Many of us experience life as something that happens *to* us rather than *through* us. When we are made redundant, get ill or go through divorce, we often think that we're the victims of such misfortunes. In a conversation, when someone shouts at us, puts us down or turns away, we think there's nothing we can do. But by becoming conscious, creative participants in the unfolding of our lives, we can change everything.

By more "conscious", I do not mean more cerebral. Overthinking will undermine a conversation even further. Nor do I mean becoming more self-conscious, for that provokes anxiety. What I'm talking about is becoming more aware, more alert and more active in a way that increases our sense of vitality. It's about engaging with the other person and with life so that we feel fully alive.

Having a Big Conversation is not something that most of us are born knowing how to do. Because talking is such an everyday activity, we might assume that we should automatically be able to find our way in encounters with others. Not so. Many of us find it challenging to keep a conversation flowing, particularly when we're at a critical juncture in our life. Many of our problems arise "between" us and can only be resolved by consciously navigating the "between", which is not an easy art to master.

When I was learning to drive, it occurred to me that I'd be fine without any other drivers on the road. I quickly got to grips with changing gears, applying the brakes and manoeuvring the car around a deserted supermarket car park. However, when it came to negotiating my way at traffic lights, roundabouts and junctions— in short, dealing with other drivers—it took me much longer to get the hang of it. I soon discovered that other people's driving could be unpredictable, chaotic and eccentric. I found that I needed to be constantly alert to what might happen next in the space between us.

Similarly, finding a way to have more conscious conversations with other people is something that I've had to learn how to do. The challenge has often been to interact with someone when I haven't been sure how they would react.

At some key moments in my life, I've struggled to talk with the people who were closest to me. I've asked myself many times, "What does it take to have a Big Conversation?" It's taken me over 20 years to find an answer to that question.

I believe that there are Seven Shifts to make, which I explore step by step in Part II. Below I share the story of where the ideas for these shifts came from. None of the insights appeared as a flash of intuition, but instead formed slowly as I went about my day-to-day life and then reflected on what had happened. Nor did the inspiration arrive in the neat, sequential order in which the Seven Shifts appear in this book. The living of our own life can be messy and fluid and yet I believe that it writes the book of our deepest wisdom. While the details of our lives are different, we have all felt love, fear, envy, pride, shame and sadness. We all know what it is to experience the joy and the pain of having – and not having – a Big Conversation.

Sensitization

When I was 21 (and slightly less skinny than the 17 year old I talked about in the Introduction), I was caught between a rock and a hard place. The rock was a boyfriend and the hard place was my parents. They had forbidden me to live with my boyfriend in my final year at university. My parents thought that they were right and I was wrong, and they were in charge of the purse strings. My boyfriend threatened to leave me if we didn't live together. He was a man with a great spirit of adventure but an even bigger temper. He was not shy of being verbally abusive.

I couldn't talk to either side and, like many young people trying to keep everyone happy, I ended up living a lie. My boyfriend and I moved in together, but kept it secret. The whole experience sensitized me to the costs of not being able to **call up my courage** for the conversations that were needed. I felt unable to confront my boyfriend and too nervous to talk in depth with my parents.

I became resentful of my boyfriend (more about him in a while) and a shadow was cast over my relationship with my parents. It wasn't until we eventually talked about it years later that my sadness and guilt left me. The conversation healed the chasm that had been caused by my deceit. I learned how much we suffer when we don't talk.

There were other rocks and hard places that my younger self wriggled out of. I'm sure that the people who knew me then and who are reading me now, holding forth about the importance of having conversations, will be surprised to hear how I've changed. *We teach what we need to learn* is a principle that applies as much to me as to any other person.

Something to say

The next step was discovering that I had something of value to say. It was a few years later and I was living in a remote village in Spain, in an alternative, rather anarchic community. In wandered José from Barcelona, who was into dealing drugs and breeding dogs. He was tall and thickset, with shaggy hair and a wild look in his dark eyes. The village was soon overrun with puppies who helped themselves to the contents of the various vegetable patches. This had made several of the villagers very angry. When they confronted him, José either shouted back or shut the door in their face. He was not popular.

One hot Saturday afternoon, in an attempt to stop the conflict from escalating further, 15 of us sat together – with José – outside the Common House to talk about what to do.

To begin with I didn't say much. At that time I was a smiley people-pleaser who never spoke up. I had a "story" running inside me that I hated conflict and couldn't handle it. It was only when José said, "What do you think, Sarah?" that I found my voice.

Something important had happened in the weeks before the meeting – I'd taken time to talk to José. I'd gone round to his house a few times and got to know who he was. This experience of him gave me the then-unconscious confidence to find the question that needed to be asked.

"What did you come here for?" I said.

"I came for peace and quiet".

"Have you found it?"

"Not at all."

"So what you wanted and what you've found are not the same." I searched for the truth as I felt it. I didn't want to hurt his feelings but I didn't want to swallow my words either.

"If it were me, José, I would leave." I looked him straight in the eyes and he nodded. I knew he'd heard me.

A silence fell. Maybe it was partly everyone's surprise (including mine) that I had spoken in this way. José slowly rose to his feet. He spread his hands in a gesture of acceptance. "OK," was all he said.

José left the village soon afterwards with no fuss. Life returned to the harmonious rhythm it had had before all the shouting. This experience gave me the lived knowledge that I could **surrender my "story"** and stop playing small. I learned that when I was able to **speak my truth** it made a difference to others. It also taught me about the importance of "units of contact".

Units of contact

Back then I didn't know about the concept of units of contact. I came across it at a conference I attended on Easter Saturday 2011, at Westminster Central Hall, London. Hosted by Judith Seelig, this extraordinary event, aptly named "Women on Fire", brought together women from around the world to appreciate the beauty of humanity in its female form.

The speakers were exceptional. Camila Batmanghelidjh, the founder of the charity Kid's Company, spoke of her work with traumatized young children living in London. Many of these kids have never had a stable, loving parent and the charity's centres are a kind of "aunty's house" where they can drop in and find some support.

Camila talked about her charity's research into what turned around these children's lives. They'd found that some school dinner ladies were much better than others at connecting with the kids, in terms of the little things – the glances, the "Hi"s and the hugs. The dinner ladies who'd made the most difference were those who'd had the biggest number of "units of contact" with the children, the little moments of connection that build up to have a big effect.

With José, I was the one who'd built up those units of contact. Then I was doing it intuitively, now I'm more conscious of it. Having human-to-human contact makes such a difference. When we not only make contact, but **connect with respect**, it can heal the deepest hurt.

S.E.X.

Sex is a big thing. An obvious statement, perhaps. But its implications are not so obvious, and its wider meaning is central to this book. In fact, in my understanding of sex, it's so big, it's *everywhere*. My view of sex (which I share with best-selling author Neale Donald Walsch) is that it happens whenever and wherever there is human-to-human contact. All of life is S.E.X. – Synergistic Energy eXchange. This ebb and flow, this "to and fro" movement is the basic rhythm of life and of everything in it, including conversation.

Sex is the energy exchanged when we encounter each other. The question is not whether two people are having sex, but what kind of sex are they having? What's the quality of their Synergistic Energy eXchange?

It is impossible for us not to exchange energy when we come into contact with one another. This exchange is just what inevitably happens. How the energy is used, and thus what it leads to, is up to the people who are having the experience together.

This fundamental reframing and energy-focused under-standing has made me perceive conversation in a very different and much more helpful way. When I talk with people, pro-fessionally and personally, I've become more aware of what's moving between us. I tune into how they make me feel and what I can do to keep the flow vibrant. I engage energetically with them, inviting them to join me in the dance.

My mum tells the story of taking me on visits to the swimming baths when I was about two years old. I'd potter up and down the cubicles and pull aside the orange curtains to say hello to the women as they changed in and out of their swimming costumes. Like most kids, I had no inhibitions about reaching out and exchanging energy. I am grateful to my mum for not stopping me from acting on my natural curiosity.

Now I'm older I'm reconnecting with that child in me who's happy to receive people just as they are. I gained – and then stayed in touch with – the knowledge that no one, however much of a tyrant or demon they seem, is inhuman – and that we've all got pimples, wrinkles and tickly bits when we get up close. Good for us! It's what makes us human …

Containers

When there are tough things to talk about, I've learned that **creating a "container"** is key. A container forms out of the energy exchange between people. If there are enough "units of contact", an expansive field of energy emerges, which enables the conversation to flow more easily.

My dear friend Karen is someone with whom I've learned the difference it makes to have a strong container. We've been close friends for over 10 years and have shared many joys and sadnesses.

A year or so ago, Karen came to stay with me the night before I was due to run a masterclass on dialogue for the

British Psychological Society. It was the first time she'd spent a night away from her 18-month-old son Samuel, who is also my godson. Samuel had been to hospital with breathing problems several times in recent weeks and for Karen to leave him for 24 hours was a big step.

After we'd cleared away the dinner table, Karen paused and quietly said, "I hope that what I say next won't hurt our friendship."

"What's up?" I asked, my heart starting to thump loudly in my chest.

"Well," she replied, "when I've talked about Samuel's health, you've been quick to move the conversation on. It's the most important thing going on in my life at the moment and I'm feeling really upset."

She burst into tears and I felt awful. Here I was preparing to run a workshop on dialogue for 20 psychologists and being completely insensitive to the needs of my best friend.

"I am so sorry," I said. "I'm distracted and anxious about tomorrow. Tell me what's troubling you …"

We later agreed that this short, honest conversation had actually brought us closer together. Because of the trust that's there between us, Karen was able to speak her truth without fear of our relationship falling apart. As she listened to my faltering response, I felt held by her attention, her respect and her love.

The strength of our container meant that we were able to withstand the pressure building up between us. We were able to have a potentially difficult conversation and clear the air. Heartfelt conversation takes place in an expansive emotional space where the atmosphere is appreciative. In the absence of a container, we either avoid talking or stay polite, not daring to say what's really going on for us.

Grace

Over the years I've learned that the less fear we have, the more we're able to have life-changing conversations. I didn't master fear on my own or by any conscious act of will; it came to me as a gift.

When I finally ended the relationship with my scary boyfriend, after a short while I took up with a friend of ours, a drummer. My ex, unsurprisingly, did not respond well. Being him, however, his displeasure went further. I heard that he'd spoken of "breaking the fingers off" my new partner. Whether this was true or just malicious gossip I never knew, but it did make me feel very nervous. He was angry that I'd left him without even talking about it. I'd found it tough enough to talk with him while we were together; when we broke up, I felt more scared than ever.

As previous relationships had ended in a mess, I knew how unsettling it was not to **find closure**. I felt strongly that I needed to go and see my ex to talk things through. I wanted to **send my intended message**: that I was grateful for all the adventures we'd shared and that it was time to move on.

I drove several hundred miles to find him. When I arrived at the house where he was staying, I found a note on the back door saying that he'd popped out to buy some lunch. I sat down on the step and waited. I was tired from the long journey and, although I knew we should talk, I didn't feel up to the task I'd set myself. I felt sick. My stomach churned. My hands shook.

Sitting there alone I sent up a prayer. This was a first for me, as an adult. Until then I had not been a "believer" in any sense. I'd rejected my Catholic upbringing and had been trained as a scientist. I thought that life could be explained without reference to divine intervention. But, in that moment when I felt pushed to my edge, I reached out for the God I'd known as a child, for the One I'd felt dance with me through my younger days.

Suddenly, I felt a deep sense of calm infuse me. Heaven knows where it came from. *Heaven knows.*

When my ex returned, that envelope of peace stayed with me. We cried and hugged and talked. We let each other say our piece and be sad; we listened and let go.

I learned that day that when our intention is pure and clear, the universe brings us power. When we can't go any further on our own and we ask for help, grace pours in and clears the way for a conversation.

Changing our conversations

As I look back on my journey, I can see how much these conversations have transformed me. They've challenged my sense of who I am and given me a deepened appreciation for a larger reality. I hope that they've made me a better, kinder, more aware human being.

I've also changed how I handle conversations. I've become more honest, particularly about how I'm feeling. I'm more aware of how conversation keeps my relationships alive. I take more responsibility for how I'm showing up when I encounter another person and for the energy that I bring to our exchange.

I've come to appreciate that conversation is not just talk. It is a meeting place. Although we are housed in separate bodies, conversation is where our inner worlds come together. It is through dialogue that we become intimate with each other and our souls reveal themselves. A simple conversation can take us to the edge of the sacred – sat at the kitchen table, in the garden or at the office.

When we make these shifts – call up our courage, create a container, intend the message we send, connect with respect, speak our truth, surrender our story, find closure – it changes everything. Conversations that seemed impossible become possible. Let me share with you how ...

Part II

The Seven Shifts

CHAPTER 4

Shift 1 –
Call up your courage

*"I learned that courage was not the
absence of fear, but the triumph over it."*

Nelson Mandela

Many of us find talking about what matters deeply to us very daunting. A Big Conversation often calls for a great deal of courage. Whether we need to speak our truth, express how we are really feeling or stand up for ourselves, courage is what enables us to "stay in the room" and talk.

We all have courage. Rather than acquiring it, we need to cultivate it. Just as an athlete strengthens his or her muscles ready to run a marathon, the more we practise being courageous, the easier it becomes.

It helps to weigh up the risks and benefits of having that Big Conversation compared with not speaking out. Somewhat paradoxically, it is also worthwhile taking a good look at what scares us. When we understand our fears, they weaken and we can then free ourselves from their grip.

Courage is not bravado or recklessness. A courageous conversation means speaking from the heart, being sensitive to the other person and being willing to listen. All of this takes guts. When someone says something we don't like or don't want to hear, we may have to hold our nerve rather than turn away.

Being courageous in conversation also involves listening to ourselves. We all can find it challenging to reflect on our lives. We keep ourselves busy to avoid the silence in which our anxieties may overwhelm us. Facing our fears and finding the courage to talk is what this chapter is all about.

Tough talking

You've been living with your partner for several years. You've shared joys and challenges and pooled your domestic and financial resources. You miss the deep and meaningful conversations you used to have, but choose not to dwell on it. Unexpectedly, a critical situation arises that calls for a more substantial conversation. Your partner, however, doesn't want to talk. You feel fearful about bringing up the subject and don't know how to get started. Without the conversation, you are concerned for your relationship, your well-being and your future.

Mary knows exactly how this situation feels.

Mary is a bubbly, out-going, fun-loving 55 year old. She's been building a new life for herself since being widowed 10 years ago and since her retirement from her job as a marketing manager. After five years on her own, Mary met a wonderful man who had also been bereaved and was still living in his family home in south Wales. Quiet, kind and caring, Thomas was enjoying his retirement after a long and successful career as a bank manager.

After an exciting two years of sharing their common interest of travelling, Mary and Thomas got engaged. Mary moved to south Wales and bought a half share in Thomas's house. She invested a considerable sum of money building an extension and making the house their home in anticipation of getting married. As they both had grown-up children, the couple had "mirror wills" drawn up. They wanted to ensure that, when one of them died, the survivor would inherit the other half of the house. Upon the death of the second partner, the property would then be equally divided between Mary's daughter and Thomas's son.

Two years after they set up home together, Thomas was diagnosed with terminal cancer. He was given nine months to live and went into a state of deep shock. Although he was very distressed, he encouraged Mary to spend a few days visiting her elderly mother over Christmas, as this was a family tradition.

When Mary returned home, she saw a letter addressed to Thomas on the kitchen table. Mary recognized the name of the solicitor as it was the same firm that had prepared their wills. When she handed Thomas the letter, he put it to one side and said, "Leave it."

Mary felt very troubled. Her gut instinct told her that Thomas had changed his will without discussing it with her. A few days later she decided to take matters into her own hands and she read the now opened letter. It confirmed her worst fear. Without consulting her, Thomas had changed his will so that when he died, she would now own only her half of the house and not the whole property as originally agreed.

Mary felt betrayed, hurt and angry. She was acutely aware that the two of them needed to talk. However, every time Mary tried to have a conversation about the house, Thomas would shut down by changing the subject or pretending not to hear.

Over the years, Mary had observed that Thomas would often avoid having difficult conversations, including with his own son.

She knew that it would have to be her that initiated the conversation, but she felt at a loss as to how to get it started. Thomas was comfortable dealing with facts and figures, but when it came to anything emotional, he steered well clear.

Mary was also afraid that a conversation might make matters worse. Thomas didn't know that she had found out about his changed will by looking at his letter from the solicitor. She let time go by, hoping that justice and fair play would bring things to a conclusion. When the conversation was still not happening three months later, Mary came to me for some coaching.

"I'm really scared to talk with Thomas," Mary confessed. "He's a dying man and I want to be compassionate, but I also want to ensure that I don't lose what I'm entitled to. How can I find the courage to have what feels like the biggest conversation of my life?"

What follows is the answer we found to that question, step by step.

Access your courage

When faced with a Big Conversation, our challenge is to call up the courage we have deep inside. Even when we are trembling with fear, there is a spirit of boldness within. It is this very spirit that makes a toddler stand up and try to walk each time she topples over. Our resolve to reach out and talk to another person can certainly be suppressed by fear but, if we dig deep enough, we will find it.

There is no cookbook approach to accessing our courage for a Big Conversation. We can't follow any recipe with guaranteed results. What we can do, however, is to look back at our own lives and previous conversations, as this can equip us to move forward with more confidence, conviction and *cojones*. In certain moments, we have all shown and known our strength – and we can choose to know ourselves as courageous *now*.

When I first met Mary, she was very upset by her challenging circumstances. She wept as she told me of how betrayed she felt because Thomas has changed his will without talking about it first.

"Not only am I going to lose my partner," Mary said through her tears, "but I feel my livelihood's at stake. If I don't have a Big Conversation with Thomas, it's going to affect my quality of life for the rest of my days."

I listened quietly. I knew that I couldn't fix the situation or take away the sorrow, so I simply sat with Mary and let her talk. Sometimes, the best we can do when someone is distraught is to be an emotional sponge and soak up some of the sadness. When Mary was a little steadier, I explained an exercise that could help her remember when she had called up her courage in the past. Her response was quick and direct.

"But I don't have any courage. That's for people who climb mountains. I couldn't do that!"

I responded that I believed that we all have had to step out of our comfort zone at some times in our lives. When we reflect on these instances, we can see what strategies have worked well for us in the past and we can then apply them in the present. This enables us to access our courage in a way that feels right for us, rather than by following any formula.

I encouraged Mary to complete the Backtrack exercise (see Part III, pages 211–12). She drew a timeline of her life from birth to the present day and identified the turning points when she'd shown that she'd got "steel in her spine". She also identified the times when she'd felt unable to face her fears. We can learn as much from the times when we failed to call up our courage as from the times when we succeeded.

At our next session, Mary and I discussed the occasions when she'd previously been able to move out in the face of fear. Three strategies she'd used well stood out:

- **Support from friends.** Instead of "going it alone", at
key points in her past Mary had found it beneficial
to speak with a close friend. Talking through her
situation had given her a different perspective, as
she realized that others had faced similar challenges.
When Mary felt accompanied, she felt more confident.

- **Drawing on a Higher Power.** While she wasn't religious,
Mary's spirituality was important to her. She had
successfully used a powerful prayer to steady her nerves
before presentations at work. Mary would say to the
universe, *"You have given me these gifts. If I'm going to
use them, I need your strength. I do this in your name."*
This prayer had enabled her time and time again to, in
her words, "float gracefully through any situation".

- **Writing a letter.** Because Mary sometimes found
it hard to express her emotions, she'd learned that
putting them on paper helped to clarify what she was
feeling. When she wasn't afraid of being interrupted,
Mary could express herself succinctly. She'd once sent
a letter to someone before having a Big Conversation,
which enabled her to cover what she needed to say so
that she didn't lose her nerve when they talked.

Becoming more conscious of these tried-and-tested strategies,
Mary started to see what she could do to talk with Thomas. "I
didn't think I had any courage," Mary said, thoughtfully. "But
now I can see that I've been summoning my courage for years
without realizing it."

Although the conversation with Thomas was a bigger
challenge than she had ever faced before, identifying how she
had shown her strength in the past helped Mary to shift to feeling
more positive.

"I'm starting to think that I can do this!" Mary declared, and I, too, knew that she could.

Name your fears

Courage is not the absence of anxiety, but moving out in the face of fear. Being specific about our fears, whether of rejection, loss or pain, helps to diminish them. Identifying what we're afraid of may not dissipate the dread completely, but it does help to loosen us up. And when we are no longer gripped by foreboding, we are better able to step into a Big Conversation.

Naming our fears enables us to get a handle on them. To "understand" something is to "stand under" it. This means taking a good look to see it for what it is. When we are specific about what's causing us consternation, we may find the fear is not as fearful as we'd thought.

Mary had been bereaved before and knew all too well how devastating loss could be and how long it could take to come to terms with it.

"I'm not just upset, I'm terrified," Mary shared with me. "I'm about to lose the place that's become my home. The potential for things to go wrong is enormous. I'll be devastated enough when Thomas dies, without a whole load of other grief to worry about."

I could understand Mary's fear that talking with Thomas might make matters worse, given that she'd found out about him changing his will in secret. However, at her age Mary also felt that she needed to take care of herself financially and couldn't afford to make any mistakes. I was concerned her fear would disable her and prevent her from having the conversation.

As gently as I could, I suggested that we explore what was making her so afraid. Returning to the Backtrack exercise, we revisited the times when she'd backed away from being bold, to see what Mary could learn from these experiences. If she knew what had held her back previously, she could make a different choice this time. The following factors came to light:

- **Fear of rejection**. Maintaining a harmonious relationship, particularly with her partner, had always been very important to Mary. When there was a risk of upsetting Thomas, she always tended to back down. Beneath this "treading softly", however, was a fear of being abandoned. Giving a name to this made Thomas's possible rebuff easier to cope with, as Mary realized that she was going to be on her own after his death whether they talked or not.

- **Fear of feeling guilty.** Mary had avoided having difficult conversations in the past when she thought she would be seen as too tough, detached or aloof. She was concerned that Thomas would see her as lacking compassion if she instigated a difficult conversation when he was so close to the end of his life. Naming this fear helped Mary to see that, even if he did think this, she could be clear inside about her own motives.

- **Fear of getting it wrong.** As far back as her school days, Mary had often felt foolish when she'd given a wrong answer or made a mistake. Now she was afraid that Thomas might feel hurt and betrayed if she spoke out. However, when she looked at this fear more closely, she saw that *without* the conversation, she would stay feeling hurt and betrayed. Calling out this fear enabled Mary to see this choice more clearly.

Left unexamined, fear often prevents us from reaching out because we believe, like Mary, that it could make matters worse. The problem is that the need to communicate doesn't go away. As Carl Jung, the great Swiss psychologist said, "What we resist, persists." However, naming and understanding our fears loosens their grip and allows conversation to come more easily.

Weigh it up

Courage is all about stepping out into the unknown. It involves us accepting that there are risks in starting a Big Conversation *and* that there are risks in staying silent. It can be a great relief to become clear about the appropriate route to take. When we are quietly confident about our decision to talk to the other person, our courage comes online.

To help Mary reach a clear decision, I suggested that she complete the Trade-off exercise (see Part III, pages 213–15). This would enable her to explore, in full awareness, the two options: (1) have the Big Conversation, or (2) stay silent. Sometimes not talking is the right decision, and when this decision is *conscious*, there is a sense of relief, peace and ease. When talking is the right decision, knowing this means that we can call up our courage more easily. Mary's completed Trade-off exercise is shown in Figure 1.

Mary worked in a clear sighted and systematic way through the risks and benefits of talking with Thomas. Then she went home to sleep on it. At our next session, she shared her decision with me. "I've come to the conclusion that a courageous conversation is called for," Mary said. "Although the idea of talking with Thomas scares me, the risks of silence are so much greater than the risks of speaking out. I stand to lose much more if I don't face my fears."

Mary was willing to make the necessary sacrifice to have the Big Conversation. She would risk some short-term discomfort for a longer-term gain. While things between her and Thomas might "get worse before they get better", talking offered Mary a greater chance of finding peace of mind, resolving her financial situation and creating a future she wanted.

Figure 1 – Mary's trade-off	
Have the Big Conversation with Thomas	
Risks	**Benefits**
• It may make the situation worse. Thomas doesn't know that I looked at the solicitor's letter and might get angry. • I would have to face up to the reality of what he's done by changing the will and that could be painful. • Thomas could get very upset and I'd find that hard to deal with.	• It will clear the air and get the dialogue going. It will feel like a huge relief. • I will be able to state my case and voice my concerns. • We might be able to get to a win—win resolution. • I would avoid having regrets later about saying nothing.
Stay silent	
Risks	**Benefits**
• My uncertain legal status means I could lose my home. • I could lose a considerable amount of money. • Nothing will change and I will feel terrible	• Pretending not to know Thomas has changed his will brings me short term relief. • Not rocking the boat means that I can get through each day without confrontation, which I hate. • I don't have to get stirred up and deal with the emotional fallout.

Build a bridge

A true conversation has to be mutual. It is only when we genuinely exchange our thoughts and feelings with each other that an encounter becomes a dialogue. For this to happen, we have to be open to "meet" the each other as the unique people we are. Given that we can be very different, a Big Conversation calls for some generosity of spirit.

Before asking, "Can we talk?", it helps to think through how to draw the best out of the other person. Recognizing and respecting the other person's way of showing up in a conversation enables us to avoid a "mismeeting". This is the term Martin Buber, the philosopher and theologian, uses for a conversation in which we talk but have no real contact. By contrast, a Big Conversation opens us up, changes our lives and leaves us feeling complete because of the depth of connection we've had with the other person.

As our coaching progressed, I sensed that Mary and Thomas were poles apart personality-wise. I found myself wondering whether their differences might be contributing to their difficulty in talking to each other. Whereas Mary was happy to spend an evening chatting with friends on the phone, Thomas would much prefer to be at the computer reading the latest financial bulletins. Mary observed that if Thomas had paid the same attention to their conversation as he had to his online bank account, they'd never have ended up in this situation.

"I just want 10 minutes of his time so he listens to what I have to say and how I feel," Mary told me as she recounted another failed attempt to communicate with Thomas.

I decided to ask her some questions to help her to understand better how she could "meet" Thomas more successfully.

"What's Thomas like when you talk together?" I enquired. "How is he different from you?"

"He's quiet and reflective whereas I'm more outgoing," Mary replied. "He listens more than he talks whereas I like to think out loud".

It struck me that Mary was describing a classic case of an extravert and an introvert trying to talk to each other. While we are all unique, there are some clear patterns that play out in conversation relating to certain personality preferences. I felt that if Mary (an extravert) could appreciate how Thomas (an introvert) conversed differently, she'd be more skilful at engaging him in dialogue. These differences are summarized in Figure 2.

Figure 2 – Extraverts and introverts in conversation	
Extraverts	**Introverts**
• Energized by conversation so like to keep it pacey • Think as they speak by articulating their thoughts aloud • Act quickly and can get distracted and impatient	• Energized by silence and solitude so may find conversation draining • Think before they speak so need time to gather their thoughts • Can be slow to get involved as they like to sit back and observe

Mary said that these different styles sounded like an accurate reflection of her and Thomas. She said she felt it would be important to enable Thomas to prepare for the conversation by giving him time to gather his thoughts.

Thinking back to how she'd called up her courage in other conversations, Mary mused, "I could write him a letter.

"I know it's vital to talk to get clarity, but I think giving him a letter first will help Thomas to hear what I've got to say. And I'll be able to think about what I really need to communicate, rather than trying to work it out in the moment."

Mary's idea sounded good to me. I felt that writing a letter as a prelude to the Big Conversation would help to slow Mary down, as well as being kinder to Thomas. Their time to talk was coming closer.

Let your heart speak

Courage is about striving toward what is noble. To act courageously, we need to let our heart speak its gentle wisdom. The English word "courage" comes from the French *coeur*, meaning heart. The easiest way to find our courage is not by intellectualizing about it, but by listening to our heart.

Before Mary reached out to Thomas with her letter, I was keen that she take some time to go inside herself. I was concerned that, in her writing, she might lay out all the financial facts and figures without saying how she was *feeling*. For her to really connect with Thomas, a dying man, she needed to open her heart and speak from there.

A Big Conversation also calls on us to *listen* – to ourselves and to the other person. Once we're able to hear the voice of our own soul, we will be better able to hear what the soul of another has to say. With this in mind, I suggested that Mary complete the Inner-view exercise (see Part III, pages 216–18). This involved her going within herself to find out what the courageous voice inside had to say.

At our next coaching session, Mary shared with me that her "conversation with Courage" had been quite unlike anything she'd ever experienced before. As she listened to the quiet voice within, she could feel her strength stirring inside.

"It's becoming clearer and clearer that talking with Thomas is the way forward," she said. "More than that, I have a sense that all will be well."

Listening to her own inner wisdom helped Mary to kindle her courage and have the Big Conversation that would change her life.

Take action

When we act courageously, we feel alive. We may be walking into the unknown, but we choose to feel exhilarated, not just scared. It is only by making a bold move that we know ourselves to be courageous. When we are able to talk and listen openly with nothing left unsaid, life can flow in its fullness.

In the build-up to a Big Conversation, it is helpful to go inside ourselves and seek our own counsel. Once we find clarity within, however, it is time to reach out to the other person. Inviting someone to talk is a decisive action.

I was keen to support Mary in seeing this through. Working

up our psychic muscle often doesn't come easily. We might know what we need to do, but actually doing it is another matter. We may come up with all sorts of excuses as to why now is not the right time or why the other person isn't ready. Mary was no exception.

"But I don't know how to get started," Mary said, as we talked about her writing a letter to Thomas.

"Getting started is often the hardest part," I replied. "However, once we make our first move, then we usually find some momentum to keep going.

To help Mary on her way, I suggested that she set herself a S.M.A.R.T. goal, one that is Specific, Measurable, Achievable, Realistic and Time-bound. I would then hold her accountable for what she had said she would do.

"My goal is to write a letter to Thomas, confessing that I know about his changed will, describing how I feel and outlining the facts," said Mary. "I'll also include the questions that I need answered and a clear request for us to talk."

After a pause, Mary continued. "I've decided that what I'm *not* going to do is to try and analyze why Thomas decided not to honour the contract he made when he was in good health and life stretched out before him. I'm going to focus on how we can move forward in a way that causes least pain for us all".

"Good," I said. "Writing a letter is a very specific action that will help the conversation to happen. When will you have written it by?"

"This time next week," Mary replied, her voice sounding strong. "But I think there's something missing.

"I think it should be a Very S.M.A.R.T. goal, with the "V" standing for 'visualizable'. I know that if I can see myself doing something in my mind's eye, then it'll get done."

I invited Mary to close her eyes and see herself writing the letter. I asked her to describe how she wanted to feel as she saw herself pick up the pen, as if she were feeling that way *right now*.

"I'm feeling calm, confident and centred," said Mary, with her eyes still closed.

After a few more minutes imagining herself completing the letter and handing it to Thomas, Mary shared an insight she'd had.

"It's a bit like setting my 'sat nav,'" Mary said. "My destination in writing this letter and talking with Thomas is a place of calm, confidence and centredness. I've decided that's where I'm heading."

With her sat nav set, Mary and I discussed what she would say to Thomas when she handed him the letter.

"I think it would be helpful for you to say a little of what the letter's about," I suggested. "Thomas can then choose when's the best time for him to open it, as he might like to wait until he's got time to digest what it says.

"I'd also suggest you are clear about when you'd like a response by," I went on. "Then the situation will be less likely to drift."

Mary paused. "I can do this," she said. "The time to talk has come and I don't feel scared any more."

Hearing those words, I knew Mary had called up her courage ready for the Big Conversation.

Opening the door to dialogue

After Mary had written the letter, she placed it in an envelope and addressed it to Thomas. She had to decide when to give it to him as he was undergoing radiotherapy and she was mindful that it was a very challenging time for him.

After a couple of days Mary decided the time was right to call up her courage, stand in her truth and give the letter to Thomas.

"Thomas, I'm very concerned about the situation with our wills and I have a lot of questions about the meaning of the legal jargon." Mary took a deep breath as she continued.

"I realize this is a very difficult situation for us both, so I've put all this in writing for two reasons. Firstly, so you can read it quietly and reflect upon my questions and your answers, and secondly because I'm feeling so emotionally distraught about the situation. Writing this letter has given me time to prepare the questions I need to ask."

Mary paused before adding. "After you've had an opportunity to go through it, please let me know when you would be ready to talk about it."

Thomas averted his eyes as he took the letter from Mary and briefly said he would look through it.

Each day Mary hoped that Thomas would say he was ready for the Big Conversation. After several days had gone by, Mary knew in her heart that once again she would have to call up her courage and ask the question, "Can we talk?"

One evening Mary waited until Thomas had watched the six o'clock news, as he always did. She made him a cup of tea and said, "Thomas, is it convenient to have that talk now?" Thomas replied that it was.

Switching off the television, Mary sat down next to Thomas. She asked him, "How would you like to do this? Would you like to go through my letter paragraph by paragraph or do you prefer to work through it in your own way? I'm happy with whatever you choose".

Thomas said he would prefer to work through the letter paragraph by paragraph. So that is what they did.

As they looked together at the legal jargon, Thomas realized that he did not understand the implications of some of the wording. He suggested that Mary should make an appointment with a solicitor of her choice and ask the questions that he couldn't answer.

Mary said calmly, "That's a good idea, but I'd prefer it if you'd agree to come with me, so that you can hear the answers for yourself. Then we'll both be clear about what's involved." Thomas agreed he would do this.

Mary breathed a big sigh of relief. By following what she had learned in her coaching, she'd presented her concerns in a way that Thomas had been able to understand. She'd found her way to express herself with clarity, compassion and composure. At last it seemed that the terrible Sword of Damocles that had been hanging over her head and paralyzing her with fear for several months was to be removed.

After their visit to the solicitor, Thomas agreed to change his will to give Mary a better deal. While he did not revert to the original mirror will, he did extend the period of time that Mary could stay in the house after he died, from two to four years. After then, however, she would still have to sell the house and give half the proceeds to Thomas's son.

As Thomas became progressively more ill, he reflected on the situation further. He shared with Mary that he realized that he had not honoured his commitment and had gone back on his word. He was on the verge of asking Mary to get the solicitor to come to the hospice to reinstall the mirror will, but died before the visit could take place.

Mary was left feeling extremely vulnerable. She shared her concerns about whether she'd be able to buy a new house with a friend, who suggested that she should explore whether she had sufficient grounds to contest the will. After taking legal advice, Mary felt both sad and relieved to learn that she had a strong case. She'd always disliked conflict and was aware how contesting a will could damage relationships. She'd always got on well with Thomas's son but now, she told herself, she was fighting for her future well-being.

Mary realized that, in order to start the legal procedures, she'd have to apply what she'd learned from her Big Conversation with Thomas. The last time I saw Mary she was preparing documents for her solicitor to take to court, having summoned her spirit of boldness, managed her emotions and decided to take action. Mary told me that time had been a great healer and that she was feeling philosophical about all that she'd been through.

"It feels like my life lesson," Mary shared with me. "Now that I've learned how to call up my courage, I know that it's there for me to use whenever I need it".

Summary

Calling up our courage is essential for a Big Conversation. Courage is not something we have to acquire; it is something that we already have and can call forth. The following steps will help you to reach beyond your comfort zone and talk:

1. **Access your courage**. Look back at the times in your life when you've shown some strength. Identify what helped you in the past, to see what strategies you can apply to your current situation.

2. **Name your fears**. Take a closer look at what's making you anxious. Be specific. Identify what the fear is – for example, it might be of rejection, loss or pain. Become aware of how your fears become smaller when you understand them.

3. **Weigh it up**. Think through the risks and benefits of having the conversation and staying silent. Let yourself sleep on the decision. Become clear about your reasons for talking – or not talking.

4. **Build a bridge**. Reflect on how you can "meet" the other person where they are. An introvert will benefit from time to gather their thoughts before speaking. An extravert needs to talk to work out what they think. Flex your style to adapt to theirs.

5. **Let your heart speak**. Take some quiet time to go within. Hear what the courageous part of you has to say. Listen to this voice of wisdom inside. Ask questions and let it speak without judging or rejecting. Embrace the messages that it brings.

6. **Take action**. Decide what your next move is, set a deadline and then *do it*. Ask someone to check with you later that you've done it. Use the power of your imagination to visualize yourself taking action in the way you'd like.

The courage to talk

"Courage is not simply one of the virtues, but the form of every virtue at the testing point," wrote C.S. Lewis. Inner strength is a quality that we all need in order to navigate our way through life and difficult conversations.

Many of us find courageous conversation hard. Research by Performance Coaching International in 2008 confirms how widespread this problem is. In a survey of 750 managers in public, private and voluntary sectors, 70 percent said that they were unable or unwilling to have the "courageous conversation" needed to address poor performance in their staff.

The managers gave two main reasons. Firstly, there was an underlyng fear of having such conversations. Secondly, there was a lack of understanding about how to go about them.

Having some know-how makes a big difference. When we're able to call up our courage for a conversation, we can resolve issues, create change and move on. It also makes us feel good. "Joy is the emotional expression of the courageous," wrote Paul Tillich, the theologian and philosopher, in his 1952 classic *Courage to Be*.

CHAPTER 5

Shift 2 –
Create a container

"I felt it shelter to speak to you."

Emily Dickinson

conversation is often the way we begin our interactions with another person. If that goes well, we form a friendship. And if that goes well, we experience a deeper sense of connection or oneness with that person. Good relationships grow out of good conversations. Once we appreciate this, we are more likely to pay more attention to how we talk together and how we create a "container" for the talking.

The reverse is also true. Broken relationships stem from aborted conversations. When we don't find a way to talk to each other, hurts fester, resentment grows and our sense of separation increases. Families have fallen apart because of not talking, couples have collapsed and nations have gone to war. Hidden inside every conflict is a conversation that hasn't happened.

Before we try to heal a relationship through a conversation, we have to prepare the ground. It is essential to have our own container where we can hear ourselves think, feel what it going on inside us and work out what we need to say to the other person. Once we have done this inner work, we are in a better position to reach out and talk.

When we talk together, being in a robust container with the other person also makes a huge difference. We can take a risk to say what really needs to be said. A disagreement can disturb a relationship without rupturing it. We are able to ask questions and explore issues that will help to close the chasm between us.

Containers don't just appear, but have to be consciously co-created. They emerge out of us coming together in an atmosphere of safety, honesty and appreciation. Only when there is an expansive emotional space do we feel safe to open our hearts, bare our souls and let our minds meet. Knowing how to reach out to someone and create a container is what this chapter is all about.

Make the space to talk

You've been out of touch with your father for years. In the absence of talking, you've become strangers to each other. You've recently felt a pull to get back in touch, aware that time is passing and your relationship with him is withering away. You feel nervous and excited at the thought of meeting up. You're also aware that you've felt this way in the past and have walked away from previous conversations with a sense of disappointment weighing heavy in your heart. Still, you feel drawn to see if you can renew your relationship with a conversation. You're not sure how to go about this or whether it's even possible, given your past experience.

Lily is facing exactly this challenge.

Lily is a bright, vivacious 30 year old. She is personable and articulate, with a real artistic flair. She grew up in Sydney, Australia, where she became a professional painter. Her parents split up when she was six and her father moved away, after which she saw him only occasionally. Her mother has told many stories over the years of how unreliable, irresponsible and chaotic her former husband was. Lily's brother, who is two years older, has shared similar stories of neglect, having lived with his father for several months as a teenager.

Lily left Australia five years ago to go travelling and broaden her horizons. Her first stop was London to see her father, Tony. She describes her last meeting with him as difficult, disturbing and disappointing. Lily decided to put the relationship behind her and spent the next few years travelling around Europe. She led workshops on drawing, took courses on modern art in different cities and sold the paintings that she created along the way.

Lily is now at an important turning point in her life. On a recent return trip to the UK she met the man of her dreams and has decided that she wants to settle down and have a family of her own. She feels that healing her relationship with her father will help her to move into motherhood with greater peace and equanimity. Some painful memories from her childhood have started to surface and Lily wants to deal with them before they make her feel overwhelmed about becoming a parent herself.

Despite all the instability, turmoil and hurt she experienced while she was growing up, Lily feels a huge longing to reconnect with her father now she's an adult. When a good friend recently lost both her parents, it caused Lily to revisit her relationship with Tony.

"I want to explore whether our relationship can be healed before it's too late," Lily says, "but I don't know if we could have the conversation."

As she is now in the same country as Tony, Lily feels it's an ideal opportunity to establish contact again. She'd love to have his blessing on her new relationship and to be able to share her hopes and dreams with him. Lily knows she wants to talk, but doesn't know how to have a dialogue without disappointment.

"I've walked away from all our other encounters feeling confused and despondent," Lily reflects. "I want to talk with Tony but I don't want to open myself up to more hurt."

Feeling at a loss, Lily got in touch with me for some coaching. "How do I create a relationship with someone who's become a stranger to me?" she asked. What follows is the answer we found to that question, step by step.

Grow your own container

Imagine that you're walking down the street near your home. You suddenly see a good friend come toward you. As you greet each other, this person wraps their arms around you in a warm embrace. You feel sheltered, supported and completely accepted by them. For a moment you allow yourself to be fully in their presence and let their energy envelope you. Even after the hug ends you still feel "held" by them – by their attention, by their acceptance and by their appreciation of you. This is what it's like to step into a strong "container". With loved ones, creating a container can be so effortless we don't even notice it's happening.

"Container" comes from the Latin *con*, meaning "with", and *tener*, meaning "to hold". The essence of a container is, therefore, the sense of being held. There are many things, in addition to people, that can provide us with this sense of shelter. We can be "held" by our ancestry, family values, religion or worldview. There may be physical places we go to where we know we can drop our concerns and breathe more easily. There are things that we do that help to bring us back to ourselves, such as writing, singing, dancing, drawing, gardening, walking, meditating and daydreaming.

Before having a Big Conversation, it is important to be centred in our own being. When we have a strong container of our own, we feel grounded and can hear ourselves think beneath the noise of our chattering minds. We can feel what's moving through our body, whether it's sadness in the pit of our stomach, fear fluttering in our chest or joy bursting from our heart.

Coming into our own container involves slowing down, turning away from distractions and moving into our own space. We bring the shutters down on the outside world and become more sensitive to what's going on inside. Once we are centred in ourselves, we are available to meet the other person and have a life-changing conversation.

Before the encounter with her father, I felt it was important for Lily to strengthen her own container. I was concerned that if she didn't take the time to do this, she might not have the steadiness and sustenance needed to meet Tony in a new way.

"Meeting my dad again makes me feel very vulnerable," Lily shared with me. "I desperately want to connect with him, but don't want to be disappointed again."

I encouraged Lily to do the Homepages exercise (see Part III, pages 219–21). This involved using her breathing to still herself, both physically and mentally, and doing some reflective writing or "journaling" to help her uncover her thoughts and feelings. We then talked through what she'd written, to help her prepare for reaching out to Tony.

"I can't let this relationship slip away any longer," Lily said. "I've decided to send Tony an email. I'm going to say that I'd like us have a conversation, and ask him, 'Can we talk?'"

As a result of becoming centred, Lily was clear why the conversation with Tony mattered so much and how she was going to get it underway.

"It's been four years since we've exchanged emails," Lily shared, "and six years since we last saw each other. It's time I reached out to talk."

A week later Lily had some good news. She'd received a reply to her email sooner than she'd expected: Tony was willing to meet up and talk! Lily knew that she couldn't make the conversation happen on her own, but she now understood that strengthening her own container had helped her to sow the seed of a successful dialogue.

Decide what not to say

In a conversation we do not have to convey every single thought that we have about someone or the situation at hand. There are things that we might say that could cause more harm than good. Once spoken, we cannot take back our words. If we're clear about what is best left unsaid before we enter a conversation, we are less likely to find these things tumbling out of our mouths in the heat of the moment.

Early on in our coaching and in the safety of *our* container, I encouraged Lily to voice all the things she *might* say to Tony if she were to hold nothing back. Out came all the anger of feeling abandoned, all the sadness of feeling separated from him and all the hurt of feeling unloved. As she swore and shook, I did my best to stay steady and listen.

"How could he have abandoned us all those years ago!" Lily cried. "He's messed up my whole life!"

I said that given her father had left when she was so young, it was understandable that she felt that way. However, I also shared my concern that giving voice to all her judgments and accusations would shut down the conversation with Tony before it had even got started.

To help Lily to work out what might be best left unsaid, I encouraged her to complete the Discernment exercise (see Part

III, pages 222–3, and Figure 3, page 85). She wrote down all the things she wanted to blame and judge her father for, without censoring herself. We then reviewed what she'd written so she could make an informed choice about what to "bracket".

Bracketing refers to consciously setting aside our "stuff". It is a powerful practice because it helps to make us more available to talk. Instead of filling the space with our objections, we say only what needs to be said and leave room to hear what the other person has to say.

When we talked through what was best left unsaid, Lily could see that some things were to do with the "there and then" of her relationship with Tony, rather than the "here and now". This didn't mean that Lily wouldn't talk about the past, but that, when she did so, she would relate it to the present. Keeping the focus on what's happening *right now* helps a conversation to stay alive.

Discern what needs to be said

Deciding what to say and what to leave unsaid in a Big Conversation is a delicate balance. It is important that we stand in our truth without swallowing our words while still being sensitive to what will help keep the connection with the other person.

To help Lily to navigate this "narrow ridge", as Martin Buber called it, I gave her a couple of tools. The first was a question:

"What do you need to say that would make you feel incomplete if it were left unsaid?"

The second tool was a frame that Lily could use to think through what she might want to say. When a conversation has been a long time in the pipeline, it can be helpful to have some prompts for what we need to voice. I suggested Lily cover the:

- **"Hard truths"** – the things that she needed to say to clear the air

- **"Lost and forgottens"** – the things that she could be grateful for
- **"Never-before-saids"** – the things that she'd never expressed before

After she'd done some reflecting on her own, Lily shared with me that discerning what she wanted to say to her father no longer felt so difficult.

"Because I was able to express all my hurt and anger with you," Lily said, "I feel much clearer about what I *really* want to say to Tony."

When we take the time to express our negativity offline, what remains is more our truth than our judgment. "Talking it out" with a third party helps to keep the Big Conversation "clean".

Use humble enquiry

In a life-changing conversation, there is a rhythm of reciprocity. There is a constant ebb and flow, in which each of us gets to say what we choose and to make a response. In the dance of dialogue, we receive as much as we broadcast, we listen as much as we talk and we enquire as much as we assert.

This continuous movement from expression to receptivity creates an atmosphere that is conducive to conversation. Without this mutuality, we each stay in our own monologue rather than move together in dialogue. To generate the energy exchange out of which a container arises, there needs to be a balance between:

1. **Advocacy:** giving our opinion, making an assertion, taking a stand, voicing a desire, making a request, stating a preference and offering advice

2. **Enquiry:** asking a question, probing an issue, finding

out more, testing an assumption, querying something
and checking our understanding

As we are more likely to have been acknowledged, recognized
and rewarded for our advocacy, particularly at school and in
the workplace, we often overlook enquiry in a conversation.
We tend to focus on what we want to say, rather than invite the
other person to share their perspective. As advocacy is in our
blood, we need to consciously inject more enquiry into how we
talk together, to help us to connect with other people and expand
the conversational space.

Practising enquiry can catalyze our conversations into
life-changing ones. Without enquiry, we stay stuck in self-
absorption. Our conversation expands to the extent that we open
up to the unknown. If we are full of our own assertions, there
is little room left for the genuine questions that can transform
our encounter.

In our coaching, Lily and I explored how she could bring
in more enquiry when she had the conversation with Tony. In
their previous meetings they had sometimes run out of things to
talk about and not known what to say next, which had felt very
awkward. Lily identified the following as some of the questions
she would like to ask Tony:

- "Have you married again? Had any more children?"
- "Are you still not drinking?"
- "Did you hit people outside the family?"

Questions that take this form are known as closed questions.
These are questions that are direct, elicit specific information and
can often just be answered with a "yes" or "no". They are useful
when we need to get specific data. However, closed questions
can shut down rather than open up a conversation and therefore
need to be used with caution. I encouraged Lily to reshape her

questions so that they invited a fuller response. These are some of the open questions Lily came up with:

- "What's your life like now?"
- "How do you spend your time?"
- "What have your relationships been like with others outside the family?"

Open questions are broader and more exploratory. They usually begin with phrases such as "How do you feel about …", "What do you think about …?" and "Could you say some more about …?" Good open questions are powerful because they invite the other person into dialogue and demonstrate that we're interested in what they have to say.

"It feels good to have all these questions up my sleeve," said Lily. "I see now how I can help Tony to open up and talk." She paused. "But what if I don't like what he says in response? What do I say then?"

Lily was worried that Tony might try to lay a guilt trip on her for being out of touch for so long. When they'd met last time, he'd even ended up in tears at one point, which Lily had found very hard to handle.

Listening to Lily's concerns reminded me of a transformational question from the writings of Neale Donald Walsch. I'd used it myself at a critical juncture in one of my own Big Conversations. When the other person had been out to attack me, I'd asked:

"What hurts you so much that you feel you have to hurt me to heal it?"

When Lily heard the question, her eyes lit up.

"That feels like a 'healing arrow' that I can shoot if I need to," she smiled.

When it feels like people are attacking us, it's often because they want our attention. We think that they're fighting us, but

Figure 3 – Lily's preparation for the Big Conversation	
BRACKET **What's best left unsaid**	

Accusations and judgments

"You've messed up my whole life."

"Because you weren't around, I never felt I was good enough."

"When you left, I felt broken. No one would love someone who was broken."

"It's all your fault. If you'd have got help, we could have felt like a family.

ADVOCACY **My feelings, thoughts,** **desires and requests**	**ENQUIRY** **Open questions that I genuinely** **don't know the answer to**
The hard truths	**About me**
"I have felt angry and hurt by you and by the way you behaved as my father."	"What was I like as a baby?"
	"What memories of me make you smile?"
"I want you to acknowledge the pain you caused me, my brother and my mother when I was growing up."	
	"What kind of parent do you think I will be?"
The lost and forgottens	**About him**
"I have some happy memories of us when I was a child – when you used to massage my feet and the time you got me to help you paint the garden fence."	"What's your life like now?"
	"What kind of work do you do these days?"
The never-before-saids	**About our relationship**
"I want us to say goodbye to the past."	
	"How was our relationship for you when I was younger?"
"I'd like to have your blessing on my new relationship."	
	"What were some of the good times?"

all they really want is to be heard. Asking a question that lets the other person know we're listening is one way to nip an onslaught in the bud. When we do this, the door to dialogue stays open.

Attend to the physical container

A container for a life-changing conversation has both visible and invisible dimensions. Taking care of the physical container involves deciding who needs to be there, choosing an appropriate place to meet and making sure there is sufficient time to talk. The environment in which we meet to talk can have a big impact on how a conversation unfolds.

Attending to the invisible or psychological container is also very important. This is about ensuring that the atmosphere is conducive to us conversing. We need to be conscious of the energy being broadcast as we communicate. When we feel at ease, a conversation can flow. If the tone of our encounter is tense, turgid or tedious, it chokes the life out of a conversation and breaks the container.

Turning our attention to the physical container in which she and Tony would meet, Lily and I carefully considered three key aspects:

- **Who to include** – We talked through the possibility that I might be present in case the conversation got difficult. Lily decided that, given the work we had done together beforehand, she felt sufficiently empowered with communication tools to be able to handle the conversation on her own. We agreed that she could phone me at any time during the meeting if needed.

- **The right timing** – Lily set a time limit of four hours for the conversation. This meant that there was a good amount of time to talk, but not so much she'd feel overwhelmed. She reminded herself that she could leave at any time if necessary. She suggested meeting in the middle of the day, so that she and Tony could have lunch and go for a walk together to help diffuse the intensity.

- **A suitable location** – Lily decided their rendezvous would be at a train station. She felt safer meeting Tony in a neutral, public place. She reserved a table at a nearby restaurant where she knew they would be able to talk in private without being overheard. She made sure that she arrived early at their meeting point so she could ground herself before Tony arrived.

"Now that I've thought these things through," Lily reflected, "I feel much more confident going into the conversation."

With the visible, physical container taken care of, we were now ready to attend to the invisible, psychological space.

Set the atmosphere

Creating an atmosphere for a life-changing conversation is subtle and crucial work. Sometimes we can sense the energy in a room very clearly, such as when there's been an argument and we feel that we could "cut the air with a knife". Other times we might have to plug in more consciously to read the tone of the room. Either way, the quality of the energy exchange can make or break the container in which the conversation takes place.

The tone of a conversation is generated more by what happens in the space between words than in the talking itself. We have to develop our sensitivity to what is not seen or heard but felt.

To help Lily create the atmosphere she wanted for her conversation with Tony, I suggested that she complete the Cargo exercise (see Part III, pages 224–6). Lily identified three qualities or states of being that she wished to take into the conversation and use to "charge" the container with positive energy. She wrote them down on separate pieces of paper to put in her pocket on the day, to remind herself that she was carrying these energetic provisions:

| Safety | Honesty | Appreciation |

Once she had decided how she wanted to *be* as she entered the conversation, Lily and I discussed what she would *do* that would be in alignment with this. We talked about:

- **Instilling safety** – Lily decided to say at the start of their conversation that she wanted her and Tony to agree that either of them could end the meeting at any point if they hit an impasse.
- **Staying honest** – Lily had already decided that she needed to speak some hard truths to Tony. Being true to herself also meant that Lily would ask Tony for his blessing on her new partnership even if it meant he turned her down.
- **Showing appreciation** – Lily made a conscious decision that she would thank Tony for his time and his willingness to meet. She would also express her gratitude for the happy memories that she did have from her childhood

"I'd never thought of deciding in advance how I was going to show up," said Lily, thoughtfully. "I think this will make a real difference to how we talk."

As part of the Cargo exercise, Lily also wrote down the three energies that she wanted to leave to one side when she had the Big Conversation with Tony. These were:

| Shame | Anger | Guilt |

Lily knew that she could be triggered into feeling ashamed for not standing up for herself, feeling angry at the breakdown of her family and feeling guilty for having had so little contact with her father. Now that she was more aware of being in these states, they would be less likely to disturb her dialogue with Tony.

"How will you let these energies go?" I asked.

"I don't know," replied Lily, "but I'll think of something."

At our next session, Lily shared with me how she'd taken out her paint box and painted over the words on the three cards in bright colours, so they could no longer be seen. She had decided that it was time to move on.

"It was very liberating to do the Cargo exercise," Lily told me. "Setting aside some of the pain and anger I've been feeling has really helped me. It's freed me up to be who I am right now, rather than be stuck in the past.".

On hearing that, I sensed that there was one more piece to put in place for Lily to be ready to talk with Tony.

Expand the container

Containers, as we have seen, need to be created. There is much we can do to create a conversational space, but there is never any guarantee that talking will become a life-changing conversation. Even our preparation is only a safety blanket. Once we step into the conversation, we have to let go of what we think we'll say and surrender to what's actually emerging in the here and now.

A life-changing conversation unfolds to the degree to which we *listen*. I believe that listening is the most overlooked and underrated conversational skill. We're attracted to people who listen deeply to us because in the radiance of their full attention we feel vibrant, alive and understood. When we truly listen ourselves, it helps other people to open up and speak their truth. Listening is the lifeblood of a conversation.

Lily and I talked through how she could be present to Tony. We explored how she could not only listen to what he said, but also to what he was trying to say. I shared with Lily what I have come to call the three interactive listening skills and we discussed how she could apply these to keep the conversation with Tony flowing.

Skill 1: Listening for troublesome emotions

The way you deal with "energies in motion" or "e-motions" is crucial to how a Big Conversation goes. Guilt, anger, fear and jealousy can disturb a dialogue unless they're attended to. If these emotions arose in Tony, Lily decided, she could give a simple acknowledgment such as:

- "I can understand how you could feel that way."
- "It sounds like you're really sad about this."
- "I hear your sense of regret."

Skill 2: Listening for what's trying to emerge

As true dialogue is mutual, we can never know what will arise in the space between us. A life-changing conversation is all about stepping into the realm of the unknown by allowing what is seeking to emerge to come through. Lily decided that she could articulate what she sensed was arising in the conversation with statements such as:

- "My sense is that what we're talking about here is …."
- "I may be wrong but what's coming to me is …."
- "I'm curious about whether you're also hearing …."

Skill 3: Listening for what's happening right now

Sometimes a conversation can veer off in a direction that's unhelpful or "go down a rabbit hole". When time is limited or there are important things to discuss, we may need to refocus. Lily worked out that she could bring her and Tony back to the here and now by asking:

- "I wonder how what you're talking about relates to the current situation?"
- "What similarities do you notice between then and the present?"
- "What have you learned from that experience that would help you right now?"

Life-changing conversations happen when we pay as much attention to how we're listening as to how we're speaking. Listening opens up the container so that new energies can ride in.

"I hadn't realized that I needed to pay so much attention to how I listen," reflected Lily. "It feels like it might be hard work, but if it will turn disappointment into dialogue, then I'm up for it!"

There was a buoyancy in Lily's voice that I hadn't heard before. With her new-found strength and container-building skills, she was now as ready as she would ever be for her Big Conversation.

Healing the hurt

On the day she was to meet Tony, Lily awoke feeling excited but apprehensive. To ground herself, she took a few minutes to do some journaling. As she put the cards on which she'd written the energetic provisions of safety, honesty and appreciation into her bag, Lily reminded herself to carry these qualities into her encounter with her father.

Lily arrived early at the train station where she was to meet Tony. She took a few moments to take some deep breaths. When she breathed out, she emptied herself of the shame, anger and guilt she'd felt in the past when they'd talked.

When Lily caught her first glimpse of Tony, she felt her heart beat faster. To help her to stay centred, she deliberately slowed down her walking pace as she approached him.

"Hi, Tony," Lily said, with a friendly smile. "Thanks for coming."

She suggested that they take a stroll along the river and then go for lunch. As they walked and talked, Lily asked Tony to agree that if they hit an impasse they could draw their conversation to a close. Tony was supportive and said he hoped that wouldn't be necessary.

When Lily found herself feeling confused about what to talk about, she quietly reminded herself of the things she'd decided not to say: the accusations and judgments that she'd chosen to bracket. She brought to mind the questions she wanted to ask Tony so that the conversation would flow, which it did effortlessly.

Later on, when she felt more of a connection with Tony, Lily spoke of how angry and hurt she'd felt over the years about him leaving. She was careful to balance this with asking Tony how it had been for him. As Lily listened, she started to understand how hard it had been for him to leave and the deep sense of guilt that he'd carried ever since.

In a moment of tenderness, Lily was surprised to hear herself say to Tony something that she'd never come close to even contemplating before.

"I forgive you for what happened," Lily said quietly. "I can see that you did the best you could at the time."

Tony turned to her with tears in his eyes and shared with her some stories from her childhood. She found out that he'd read to her at bedtime and bought her books to keep her amused. Lily was deeply touched. When she told Tony about her new relationship and desire to become a mother one day herself, he said he was delighted.

When Tony tried to talk about the future, Lily reigned him back in to focus on the present.

"I feel overwhelmed at the thought of an on-going relationship. I'd need some time to think about it," she said, as sensitively as she could.

As their time together drew to a close, Lily was careful to thank Tony for being willing to talk. As she walked away from their encounter, she felt tired but elated. The hurt that she'd carried over many years had been healed through that one Big Conversation.

Summary

Creating a container for a life-changing conversation is powerful and subtle work. When there is a safe and energizing atmosphere, talking together can be transformational. The following steps will help you to create this expansive emotional space:

1. **Grow your own container**. Ground yourself before you reach out to someone. Do whatever it takes – write a journal, meditate or walk. Slow down and step into your own container, where you can hear yourself think and tune in to how you feel.

2. **Decide what not to say**. Put to one side the judgments and accusations that are best left unsaid. Make a conscious decision to leave your "stuff" to one side. Bracket what is to do with the "then and there" and focus on what's "here and now".

3. **Discern what needs to be said**. Decide what you need to say to feel complete. Think through what you choose to communicate: the hard truths, the lost and forgotten things and the things you've never said before.

4. **Use humble enquiry**. Help the other person into the conversation by identifying the questions that will open them up. Articulate your curiosity in the form of broad, open questions that have an appreciative tone.

5. **Attend to the physical container**. Decide whom to include in the conversation. Choose the right timing and the length of time for talking. Make sure your meeting place is conducive to the conversation.

6. **Set the atmosphere**. Pay particular attention to the tone of how you want to talk together. Decide in advance which qualities you want to bring to the conversation. Write these down and carry them with you to remind you to broadcast this energy.

7. **Expand the container**. Listen deeply. Actively demonstrate that you're hearing the other person by using interactive listening skills: reflect back their feelings, focus on the here and now and articulate what you sense is trying to emerge in the conversation.

How the physical environment affects how we talk

Studies reported in *The Psychologist* (November 2005) reveal the impact that a classroom layout has on a conversation. Physical characteristics, such as the seating arrangement, affect how we talk together in ways we may not notice.

Students who sat in a semicircle were found to ask more questions compared with students who sat in rows. Moreover, the amount of "on-topic" discussion more than doubled when students were able to see each other. Face-to-face contact is important for dialogue, as unobstructed eye contact helps us to pay attention and show interest.

Other research reported in *The Psychologist* (April 2008) shows how even something as apparently irrelevant as holding a hot or cold drink can influence our conversations. Students were asked to hold a cup of either hot or iced coffee while they answered a few questions. Next, they had a chat with another researcher. After he left, the participants were asked if they would recommend him for a job. The participants who had held the iced coffee were much more likely to say that they wouldn't recruit him, whereas those who had held the hot drink said that they would. Our environment affects us more strongly than we think.

CHAPTER 6

Shift 3 – Intend the message you send

"Your life proceeds out of your intentions for it."

Neale Donald Walsch

A Big Conversation is sometimes a threshold we have to cross to create a new life for ourselves, whether this is saying to someone that we love them, speaking out to get the job of our dreams or telling our partner that we want to let them go.

When we know that talking with someone will have a major impact on our life, and on the lives of those around us, many of us avoid the conversation. Instead, we carry on living a life of quiet desperation and of feeling uncomfortable, depressed or anxious. Breaking out of a cycle of stagnation demands energy: we have to find the stamina and self-respect to make a different choice.

When we are confronted with our own inertia, one of our greatest allies is the power of intent. This is a mighty force that can propel us forward and get us back on track. With intent, we can find a way that stretches into our future and step into talking together. Clear intent activates a Big Conversation when we so choose.

Leveraging intent also makes a real difference in the conversation itself. We speak more authentically, we challenge more respectfully and we are more aware of what's happening. As our intentions become clearer, our conversations become more potent. Finding the power within to start a new chapter by talking to another person is what this chapter is all about.

Intend to talk

You've been married for nearly 20 years, almost your entire adulthood. Your wife has been a stable, reliable and decent companion for all that time and you've had two children together. For the last 10 years you've been feeling that you've "settled" for something comfortable rather than living a life that really lights you up. You've had a couple of affairs to taste excitement again, but know that seeing other people only creates guilt for yourself and pain for your wife. You've started to imagine a new life for yourself, doing what you really love, but you are afraid to walk out into nothing ... and everything. Your wife has tried to talk with you about your future together in the hope that things will get better. You have avoided talking, as you know deep down that your heart really isn't in the marriage any more – in fact, hasn't been for some time. You know that having the conversation runs the risk of changing everything – for yourself, your wife and your family.

Pete has experienced this difficult situation.

Pete is a jovial, easy-going 40 year old with a twinkle in his clear brown eyes. Born in the East End of London to a Greek mother and an English father, he speaks with a friendly Cockney twang and there is a Mediterranean warmth and open-heartedness to his presence. With his passion for personal development, Pete is not the typical successful City property developer, having had an interest in Eastern philosophy since childhood.

Pete met Catherine when they were both 19 years old and living in the same street. Catherine was training to be a social worker and Pete was odd jobbing. Coming from a family of fiery tempers, Pete was attracted to Catherine's kind, caring nature. After three years of dating, during which she qualified as a social worker, Catherine got a visa to work in Canada and she asked Pete to marry her so they could go together. They enjoyed a year living in Toronto and then, the arrival of their first child now imminent, they decided to head back to the UK to start their family. Pete and Catherine now live in Essex with their two teenage children.

Pete describes the early days of their marriage as being friendly, happy and calm. He is quick to acknowledge how loving, devoted and dedicated Catherine has been as a wife and mother, but he says that, 20 years later, there is an air of "false happiness" between them. They avoid going to bed at the same time, so that they don't have to confront the reality of no longer having a sexual relationship. Pete misses the physical intimacy and knows that without it, he doesn't feel fulfilled. He also knows that seeing someone else is "no place to hide", as past experience has taught him that having an affair simply doesn't sustain the marriage.

In the last few years Pete feels that a "clear distance" has opened up between him and Catherine. He says that when this feeling of being disconnected flares up, Catherine wants to have *that* conversation. She wants to know the truth of the situation: will their marriage get better? His typical response is, "I don't know what to say". She gets tearful, he withdraws and she goes silent. A sense of separation sets in. As they seem unable to break out of this pattern, Pete feels increasingly resigned and frustrated. He carries on providing for his family and being there for his kids, but feels more and more desperate inside.

Pete's lifelong interest in personal development has recently taken a new turn. He's started giving evening talks and has been invited to run workshops. With his sense of calling growing stronger every day, Pete knows he has to have the conversation with Catherine about how he feels and what the future holds.

"I know I'm being 'wishy-washy' by not saying anything," Pete admits. "I just don't know what to say."

After many years of solo soul searching, Pete finally took the plunge and reached out for some coaching. At our first session he asked me, "How can I get the message across that the marriage is no longer working, without causing too much hurt?" What follows is the journey we took to find an answer to that question.

Power up

Our intent shapes our reality. Like a stone thrown into a pond, it sends ripples out through our experience and creates change. Clear, focused, directed intent makes a particularly big splash. In conversation, we do well to scrutinize our intent before we talk, so that the message we send is the one we intend.

Early on in our coaching, Pete was in a state of turmoil. He was experiencing a whole range of different thoughts and emotions as he contemplated talking with Catherine. In some moments, he said he felt resigned, frustrated and desperate. In other moments, he was able to touch a different state, as though he were sensing the future that awaited him.

"I want to be shining my light, pitching up my highest goal and living my grandest dream," said Pete, as he described his vision of setting up a new business running personal development events.

By contrast, there were other times when Pete admitted, "I can't decide what to do. I want to make a change, but I don't know how to go about it."

In his darker moments, Pete would say, "I'm completely confused. I've no idea what's out there waiting for me. I can't see a way to have the conversation with Catherine."

Listening to Pete talk, I felt myself being tossed around with the chaos of his thoughts. I could feel his angst as he contemplated leaving his marriage and the upheaval this would create for his wife and children. I also felt concerned for Catherine, because if Pete stayed in this state of confusion, they would never be able to have *that* conversation about their future – wherever it took them.

I found myself thinking of an analogy that David Bohm uses in his book *On Dialogue* to illustrate how thought works. Ordinary thought, he argues, is often "incoherent", going in all sorts of directions. Different thoughts conflict and cancel each other out. Similarly, ordinary light is "incoherent", as the light waves go in all directions and don't build up any power.

A laser, on the other hand, produces a very intense beam of light that *is* coherent. As the light waves are all travelling in the same direction, they build up strength. A laser beam is therefore able to do things that ordinary light cannot. It can cut metal, heal the body, scan a barcode as well as light up the sky.

With this image in mind, I decided to do my best to help Pete to "power up" by becoming more coherent in his thinking. I asked him to focus on what he wanted and to find three new thoughts that would align with this. I suggested that these statements should make him feel good *and* be believable. Pete came up with:

- "I am going to honour myself and my family as best I can."
- "There *is* a way through this."
- "I've been able to have challenging conversations in the past with clients."

He wrote out these thoughts and placed them where he could see them every day. Now that Pete was lining up his thoughts in a consistent way, his Big Conversation would be more likely to happen.

Invoke intent

When we utilize the power of intent, we are tapping into a force greater than ourselves. The word intention has the same root in Latin as extension, attention and tension: *tendere*, meaning to stretch. To intend means to "stretch into". With clarity of intention we can stretch into our future as the conversation becomes an "aperture" through which the new can flow. There is an alignment between what we want and the direction in which Life wants to take us.

When our intent is clear, we no longer prevaricate about having a conversation, we face up to what we have to do. We stop hiding from the evidence that our energy levels have collapsed, our lust for life has ebbed away and our creative juices are dried up. We start ending the pretending that a relationship is OK and accept that, if we are to live our dream, a conversation is called for.

Talking with someone about how we're feeling and what we want sounds simple, but it is often not easy. When I asked Pete what he was finding most challenging, he spoke of the unknown future.

"I can see what I stand to lose, but I can't see what I might gain," Pete shared. "I know I don't want to stay where I am, but I don't know what I *do* want."

When we know what we don't want, but we don't know what we *do* want, it can be hard to find our voice. Dropping beneath the confusion to hear what our deeper self has to say is essential. It is from the depths of our being that we invoke intent. This can then give us something to hold onto when we feel at sea in our life.

To help Pete to summon his intent, I suggested he complete the Threshold exercise (see Part III, pages 227–8). This involved imagining that he was writing his autobiography and coming up with titles for the current chapter, and the next one. This is an exercise designed to bypass the machinations of the mind using the power of the creative imagination. When we can hear what our soul intends, we can start to move forward.

Once Pete had conjured up the titles of his current and future chapters, I asked him what threshold he had to cross to mark the end of one chapter and the start of the next. He wrote out the chapter titles and the line to cross on three pieces of paper as follows:

Current chapter	Threshold	Future chapter
Finding my music	Having the Big Conversation with Catherine	Playing my music

Pete looked thoughtfully at the pieces of paper laid out in front of him.

"I don't want to die with my music still inside me," he said. "I need to find a way to play my music, but first I've got to talk with Catherine."

Pete went on to say that, although he loved Catherine, he felt that she was no longer his life partner. If he was to ever begin his next chapter, he was going to have to talk with her. With his intent to have the conversation becoming stronger, we then turned our attention to how Pete could stretch even further into his future.

Find your opening

When we have a clear intent to talk with someone, the next step is knowing how to begin the conversation. Although this can sometimes feel like the most challenging moment of the whole interaction, it is also when we have most leverage to influence how the conversation will unfold.

Pete shared with me that he felt at a complete loss about what to say to Catherine. Their Big Conversation had been "on hold" for so long that he didn't know how to begin. He knew that if the conversation led to their marriage ending, this would be very upsetting and challenging for them both.

"If I knew how to get the conversation started, it wouldn't seem so daunting," he said.

As I believed that deep inside Pete *did* know how to get the conversation started, I asked my next question very deliberately.

"It's clear that you still care about Catherine a great deal," I replied. "So what could you say at the start that would demonstrate that?"

Pete paused. I could sense him searching inside for some words to say so he could stand in his own truth *and* be as compassionate as possible toward his wife of 20 years. I encouraged Pete to talk to me as if I were Catherine, so he could give voice to the actual words he might use. He said three things:

- "This is the most important conversation I've ever had in my life."

- "I'll always be there as a friend and to provide financially for the family."
- "There's no one else involved, but we do need to talk."

I shared with Pete that these felt like important messages to send at the start of the Big Conversation. While they might not take away the pain of the situation, I felt that they would help Catherine to hear what Pete had to say. The more Pete could reach out to Catherine with kindness, the more likely their conversation would be to create a positive change for them both.

Name your dilemma

One of the challenges of a Big Conversation is the dilemma of whether to have it or not. Naming this dilemma can be a powerful way to enter a conversation as it stops the indecision running around inside our head. Moreover, it signals our intention to talk about what matters deeply rather than stay skimming on the surface.

Being "on the horns of a dilemma" is an uncomfortable place to be. It refers to being unable to decide between two unpleasant alternatives as either could have bad results – rather like facing a bull with two horns, on either of which we might be impaled. The phrase itself comes from the Greek *di*, meaning "two", and *lemma*, meaning "premise".

As Pete and I explored his situation further, it became clear that he was in the grip of a paralyzing personal dilemma. Given that the conversation with Catherine could mean the end of his marriage, this was a particularly painful place to be. I felt that if Pete could see his dilemma clearly, he could then share it with Catherine to communicate how strongly he felt about the need to talk and create some change.

I suggested to Pete that he named his dilemma as if he were talking to Catherine. Using the frame "On the one hand – on the other hand", Pete laid out his dilemma in front of him:

"On the one hand"	"On the other hand"
"We've had a loving and supportive relationship for 20 years. You're a good wife and great mum. I don't want to hurt you or the kids. I don't want to lose your friendship and companionship."	"I feel that our deeper relationship has died. I no longer feel physically attracted to you and I don't think that will change. I feel our lives are going in different directions. I'm not happy and I think we both deserve more."

Sharing a dilemma with the other person in this way means that we are more likely to have a heart-to-heart than if we simply present our decision as a "done deal". Instead of unilaterally deciding, we expand the field of possibilities of what will happen next. After declaring our dilemma, we can also make the conversation a creative encounter by inviting the other person to say how *they* see the situation. When we truly meet one another in dialogue, we lay ourselves open to being changed by how we talk together.

"So," said Pete, "I've found my opening, named my dilemma and asked Catherine how she feels. What happens then?"

I reminded him that a true conversation goes where it will and can't be controlled.

Pete shared with me his concern: "How will I cope with her response when I don't even know what it will be?"

In our next coaching session we looked at how Pete could keep the conversation flowing as he took his next step into the unknown.

Expand your repertoire

Naming his dilemma was a very different way for Pete to begin a conversation. It transmitted his intent to deepen the conversation so that he and Catherine could talk about what mattered most. Without this, they were likely to keep repeating the stagnant pattern of avoidance that imprisoned both of them.

As intent is such a powerful resource in creating a life-changing conversation, Pete and I explored how he could apply it further. We took a closer look at how a conversation works so that, from moment to moment, Pete could make a more informed choice about how he interacted.

I shared with Pete that there is a structure at work in any conversation. Once we understand how this functions, it becomes easier to interact with another person in the way we intend. Drawing on the work of David Kantor, an American family therapist and organizational consultant, I described how there are four basic actions that can be made in any conversation (see Figure 4). Each action brings a different intention and a distinct quality to how we talk together:

- **A "move" brings direction** – by saying, for example, "I suggest we talk about …", "I think we should decide to …", "My proposal is that we …".
- **A "follow" brings completion** – by saying, for example, "I agree that …", "I support the suggestion to …", "Let's do as you say and …".
- **An "oppose" brings correction** – by saying, for example, "I disagree with …", "I see things differently in that …", "My challenge to that is …".
- **A "bystand" brings perspective** – by saying, for example, "I'm noticing that …", "It seems there is a dilemma here …", "What I'm observing is that …".

In a healthy, life-changing conversation all four actions are present and there is a flow between them. In a dysfunctional conversation one or more of the actions is missing and there are often repeated patterns among the actions that are present. When a conversation becomes rigid and draining, we can make

Figure 4 – The four actions and their intentions

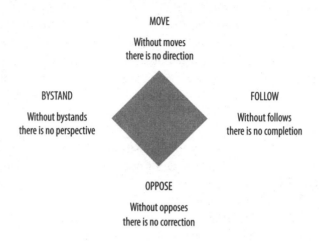

MOVE

Without moves
there is no direction

BYSTAND

Without bystands
there is no perspective

FOLLOW

Without follows
there is no completion

OPPOSE

Without opposes
there is no correction

From David Kantor, *Reading the Room: The Four Levels of
Leadership Dynamics*

it more dynamic by identifying which action is missing and bringing it in with a clear intent.

To help Pete think through how he could talk as he intended with Catherine, he completed the Repertoire questionnaire (see Part III, pages 229–31). This raised his awareness of which of the four conversational actions were his most skilful and which were underdeveloped. David Kantor has found that we typically have strengths in one or two of the actions and that we underplay at least one of them. Not using the full set handicaps us and narrows the field of possibilities into which our conversation can stretch.

Pete found that the action he was least likely to use was a bystand. He realized that when he talked with Catherine he often got so caught up in the content of their conversations that he forgot to observe *how* they were talking. This makes it very difficult to refocus a conversation when it goes off track. Learning how to pay attention to *how* we're talking together, as well as to *what* we're talking about, can take our conversation to a whole new level. Developing the ability to "dual process" in this way helps us to make a quantum leap in our dialogue.

Using the prompts given in Repertoire, Pete and I explored how he could use some bystands to bring a wider perspective to the conversation.

"Imagine that you're a fly on the wall observing yourself talking with Catherine," I said. "What might you see?"

When Pete shared with me his bystands, I suggested that he combine his observations with some enquiry to check if what he was seeing was accurate. Pete came up with:

- "I can see you're crying. Is this coming as a complete shock to you?"
- "What I'm observing is that we're starting to talk about a possible future that's scary for both of us. Shall we carry on exploring this now or take some time out?"
- "It looks like we've reached a bit of an impasse here. What do you think?."

Pete said that having these phrases up his sleeve made him feel more confident about talking with Catherine with compassion.

"I won't get so wrapped up in what *I'm* thinking and saying," said Pete. "And I've also got an idea of what to say if the conversation gets really tricky."

Taking the stance of a witness to the conversation, as well as being a participant in the conversation, helps to keep it flowing.

Provide what's missing

Pete and I also looked at which of the four actions he was *most* likely to take when talking with Catherine. While this can be an area of strength, we can also overplay this action when it would be more helpful to switch to a different one. David Kantor calls this getting "stuck" and it often undermines our ability to send the message we intend.

By completing Repertoire, Pete identified that the "stuck" action he was most likely to make when talking with Catherine was an oppose. He did this both verbally, by saying, for example,, "This isn't a good time to talk right now!", as well as non-verbally, by meeting Catherine's requests for a conversation with a silent cold shoulder. As a result, Catherine would withdraw even though she had initially been keen to talk.

Pete's oppose was having an unintended impact. While he was intending to challenge her sense of timing for the conversation, Catherine was experiencing his oppose as an attack. This "gap" between what we intend and the impact we have on another person is the root cause of many difficulties in communication.

If we don't transmit a positive, clear intention, it is more likely that we will have an impact that we don't intend. The more "spin" there is in our message, the more difficulties we will have in the conversation. For example, when Pete opposes by saying, "How can you even think of us having a conversation right now?", he is broadcasting criticism rather than a respectful challenge. Catherine then picks up on this underlying message of objection and turns away from talking.

Being skilful in conversation involves communicating with clear intention so that the message we send is what we intend. Figure 5 on page 110 shows the potential for conflict when we act without a clear intention.

Pete and I went on to explore how he could align what he really wanted to communicate with what he actually said and how he said it. Using some of the suggestions in Repertoire, Pete decided to "clean up" his opposes by:

- **Stating what he wanted not just what he didn't want.** For example, instead of saying, "I don't want to talk right now!" he could say, "I don't feel ready to talk right now. I'd prefer it if we could find some time tomorrow when I'm not so tired."

- **Giving his reasons for disagreeing.** Instead of saying, "I resent the way you won't even think about us having

Figure 5 – The gap between intention and impact		
	Positive intention	**Unintended impact**
	If this action is done well, we bring to the conversation:	If this action is overplayed, we may come across as being:
Move	Direction	Pushy
	Focus	Dictatorial
	Purpose	Impatient
Follow	Completion	Placating
	Harmony	Compliant
	Connection	Wishy-washy
Oppose	Correction	Critical
	Realignment	Objectionable
	Challenge	Attacking
Bystand	Perspective	Disinterested
	A wider context	Withdrawn
	Neutrality	Aloof

Based on the work of David Kantor

a trial separation," he could say, "I see us having a trial separation differently to the way you see it. I think it could give us the space to work out what we both want longer term."

- **Inviting challenge**. Pete could also ask Catherine to correct *his* thinking so that he was not the only one bringing in a contrasting point of view. He could say, "It would be good to hear what you make of my suggestion to separate our finances. What might I be overlooking here?"

Pete and I looked at how he could also make effective moves and follows when he talked with Catherine. We did not create a whole catalogue of specific actions with a meticulous plan for execution; such preparation would be pointless as we are never in complete control of how a conversation unfolds. What we did do, however, was work out in general terms how Pete could play each of the actions as the conversation called for them. This would help him to be flexible as he navigated his way through the Big Conversation with skill, suppleness and sensitivity.

Let go

While clear intentions contribute to a life-changing conversation, expectations detract from our ability to talk together. Being clear about what we intend while letting go of any attachment to getting a particular result is "walking the razor's edge" in a conversation. If we can find a way to do this, we remain open to new possibilities and are more able to stay centred when the unanticipated occurs.

To help Pete to surrender his own agenda, he completed the Elevation exercise (see Part III, pages 234–6). First he wrote down in a table (see Figure 6, page 113) any expectations he had for the Big Conversation with Catherine. Some of these were positive and others were negative. Pete then elevated these expectations to intentions by turning a specific outcome into a broader statement of positive intent. To help Pete to release his expectations, I suggested that he take a pair of scissors, cut along the dotted line of the table and throw away this piece of paper.

Next, Pete considered what would happen if his intentions weren't realized. We talked through what he could accept even if it wasn't his preference. Pete reviewed his intentions again and reshaped them into "acceptances". Elevating his intentions to acceptances would make him more receptive to what Catherine had to say so that their dialogue could be a true co-creation.

Pete shared with me that the Elevation exercise had helped him to look at the Big Conversation with Catherine in a new way.

"I feel less obsessed about what the outcome will be," Pete said. "I think I'll be able to go with the flow more."

On hearing these words, I knew that Pete was now as ready as he'd ever be to have his Big Conversation with Catherine.

Untying the knot

The Big Conversation, when it came, took a whole weekend. Late one Friday evening, Pete spent some time alone, sitting in his favourite chair in their living room. He felt sad but stirred to take action. He reflected on his intention to stand in his truth with Catherine and to be as compassionate as he could be. When he went to bed that night, he knew what he had to say the next day and turned over the words in his mind.

On the Saturday morning, after the kids had headed off for a sleepover at a friend's house, Pete asked Catherine if they could talk. Catherine looked a bit worried and Pete checked that she was OK to have a conversation. Catherine said she'd rather talk than be kept in the dark. Pete knew the moment had come for him to act with clear intent.

Figure 6 – Pete's expectations, intentions and acceptances		
Expectations	Intentions	Acceptances
I won't know what to say once the conversation gets difficult.	To speak my truth about how I'm feeling	It's OK to feel unsure about what to say next.
Catherine will get all emotional and start crying.	To provide Catherine with as much support as I can	I accept that Catherine might get tearful and that upsetting her will make me feel disturbed.
The conversation will give me the freedom I crave.	To decide together what's best for us as a family	I don't know what the next step is until we've talked it through.

He proceeded as intended by gently naming his dilemma and inviting Catherine to talk it through. As the conversation deepened, tears flowed, both hers and his own. He held Catherine as she cried, without trying to fix her pain or deny how desolate the situation was.

When the talking got too intense, Pete called a time out. Once they'd both gathered themselves together again, they continued to talk. As they discussed separating into different households, Catherine said how sad it made her feel but also that she'd rather know where she stood than remain in limbo indefinitely.

By the end of the weekend, Pete and Catherine had decided to stay living together for the next three months. They wanted to see if they could start to build their new relationship as friends and co-parents while Pete was still under the same roof. Even though there would be no immediate change to the domestic arrangements, they agreed to tell the kids of their decision to separate as soon as possible. In a strange way, talking together had brought them closer together even though they'd agreed to let the curtain fall on their marriage.

"We're not ending our relationship," Pete said. "We're changing its form."

Three months later Pete moved out into his own place. Catherine cried a few tears as she helped him to empty his wardrobe and pack his bags into the car. Pete reached inside to stay strong and remind himself of his intention to be true to himself while causing as little hurt as possible. He told Catherine that he'd always be at the other end of the phone if she needed to talk, and said that he'd phone the kids later to see how they were.

The transition out of the marriage was tough, but not as traumatic as Pete had imagined. He and Catherine found a way to become friends and take care of the kids while living apart. Pete's clear intent had enabled him to have a Big Conversation so that he could start to "play his music".

Summary

To create a new life, we sometimes have to step across the threshold and have a Big Conversation. Clear, focused intent enables us to move us forward and send the message we intend. These steps will help you:

1. **Power up**. Become aware where you are feeling ambivalent about what you want. Focus what you *do* want as clearly as possible. Write down some thoughts that are believable and in alignment with what you want, and look at them every day.

2. **Invoke intent**. Tune into your gut feeling. Find the fire in your belly. Get clear about what threshold you need to cross to enter the next chapter of your life. If a Big Conversation is called for, commit yourself to having this.

3. **Find your opening**. Step into the other person's shoes. Ask yourself what they need to hear at the beginning to stay in the conversation. Practise saying your opening lines so that you send the message you intend from the start.

4. **Name your dilemma**. If you find yourself in a dilemma, name it. Set the context for the other person so they better understand where you are coming from. Invite the other person to share how they see the situation.

5. **Expand your repertoire**. Decide how you can best bring in four conversational actions of move, follow, oppose and bystand. Be aware of which of the four actions you might miss and have a clear intention to bring this in "cleanly".

6. **Provide what's missing**. Be aware of where you get "stuck" in a conversation. Decide whether you can make a move, follow, oppose or bystand instead. Make your actions with as little "spin" as possible, so that your impact is as you intend.

7. **Let go**. Bring into your awareness any expectations that are lurking behind your intentions and release them. Invite in the unexpected and embrace the unknown. Identify what you can accept rather than fixating on a specific outcome.

The power of intention

Scientific research reveals how we can use the power of intention to shape our conversations and lives. In her 2007 book, *The Intention Experiment,* Lynne McTaggart describes how, at a quantum or subatomic level, everything in the universe is connected because all matter is made up of pulsating energy that is always interacting. Physical reality is therefore malleable, like an unset jelly and we can use the power of focused, directed thought to get this jelly to set.

Just as a magnetic field radiates out beyond the magnet itself, our minds are not confined to the inside of our heads. Our consciousness extends beyond our bodies through "fields" of energy that link us to each other and to the environment that surrounds us. Our thoughts, when they are conscious, coherent and focused, can ripple out through the energy field and change physical reality. Scientists have found several ways in which we can increase the potency of our intentions so that they affect physical matter. These are:

1. **Stating your intention clearly**. Use positive, specific statements expressed in the present tense, such as, "I am intending to talk with my partner" or "I have all the resources I need for this conversation". To have an impact, these statements must ring true for you. Write them down and repeat them often.

2. **Doing a mental dry run of the conversation**. Rehearse the main messages you want to give, using the actual words you would say. Imagine how the other person might respond and what you would say as a result. Pause before you make each statement to ensure that it sends the message you intend.

3. **Rehearse how you want to feel during the conversation**. Use memories to activate positive

feelings, such as relief, elation or peace. Notice where in your body you sense them as this helps to anchor these feelings in your physical reality. Practise in particular how you want to feel at the end of the conversation.

Scientists have found that working with intention lays down the tracks for having positive experiences. Using thoughts, words and feelings in a conscious, creative way is a gentle and effective way to make a difference to how we talk together.

CHAPTER 7

Shift 4 –
Connect with
respect

*"There are no elements so diverse that
they cannot be joined in the heart."*

Jean Giraudoux

The centrepiece of a Big Conversation is our connection with another person. Talking together is not just about the words that are spoken or the thoughts in our heads, but what we are holding in our hearts. When we can wholeheartedly join another human being in conversation, our lives become more meaningful and we feel more alive.

Talking with another person at a critical juncture in our life can be incredibly challenging. Giving voice to our deepest desires, particularly if they differ from what the other person wants, can make us feel vulnerable, exposed and raw. Moreover, even with our nearest and dearest, it can sometimes seem as if we are speaking different languages.

Connectivity is at the core of any conversation. However, before we can reach out to someone else, we must first be in tune with ourselves. Taking time to find the song in our own heart transforms talking together into a harmonious encounter. We can then enter a conversation and stay centred, rather than be "triggered" and walk away.

Expanding our ability to converse is pivotal to living life well. When we feel pulled to step into a different arena, whether in our work or personal life, we have to release the old before we can travel into the new. Moving on sometimes calls for a Big Conversation to free ourselves of outdated commitments. Recreating ourselves by talking with someone, heart to heart, is what this chapter is all about.

Talk from the heart

You've been a loyal, dependable wife for nearly 30 years and a committed parent for over two decades. For several years you've been feeling that you're "muddling along" as you no longer feel fulfilled in your role as caretaker of the family. The question "What about me?" keeps resounding inside as you sense that there's more to life than continuing to put everyone else's needs first. You feel pulled to explore a new line of work but you know that your family, particularly your husband, don't want things to change. You've tried to talk with him, but the conversation keeps short-circuiting. You're feeling increasingly restless, unfulfilled and empty. You want to follow your heart, but are afraid others will feel betrayed if you do.

Vida has had to deal with this challenge.

"I don't want to be here," was the first thing Vida said to me when we met. When I asked her what she meant, she replied,

"I just don't want to be here in my life or even in the UK. I feel as though I'm treading water. My life doesn't fulfil me anymore."

Vida feels she is at crisis point and has thoughts of running away. "I can't just up and leave," she whispers, with tears in her eyes. "I have to say something to my husband and kids, but I don't know how to say what's really going on inside. The situation's so difficult, I don't know how to reach out and connect with them."

Vida is a down-to-earth, practical and intelligent woman in her late forties. Her passion for the outdoors life is reflected in her glowing complexion and strong, sturdy body. Born in the UK to Spanish parents, she has lived just outside Southampton for over 25 years. Vida enjoys channelling her creative energies into gardening, a hobby that brings her a small income so that she's not entirely financially dependent on her husband. Their two children, a son and a daughter in their early twenties, have both left home but still visit regularly.

Vida met Alex, who is 10 years older than her, when she was 19. Vida describes Alex as offering her a safe harbour when she was heartbroken after splitting up with a boyfriend. Alex's steady presence made her feel reassured, protected and well looked after. Three years after meeting they were married. Their shared love of hill walking gave them a common interest and the future looked rosy.

As time passed, however, Vida realized that she was missing the passion she'd felt in her previous relationship. Things came to a head about a year ago when Vida unexpectedly met a man whom she felt to be a true soulmate. "I was bowled over by him," Vida confided. "He opened my eyes to a whole new life, full of exciting possibilities."

The encounter re-ignited Vida's lifelong passion for "re-greening planet Earth". They talked about starting a business together to plant trees in deforested areas around the world. The magnetic attraction that she felt both to him and to starting her life's work was so strong that she came very close to walking out of her marriage and family life. "But my sense of loyalty drew me back," she said. "I just couldn't up and leave. It was too drastic."

Rather than keep her affair a "dark secret", Vida told Alex. He was very upset. He hardly ate, lost a lot of weight and couldn't sleep. Alex was absolutely clear that he didn't want Vida to leave so, bowing to his wishes, Vida decided to stay and try to find a way to work things out. Rows erupt between Vida and Alex from time to time, often triggered by something trivial, but then life settles down "into limbo" again.

A year on from ending her new relationship, Vida is feeling not only downhearted, but also resentful and trapped. Whenever she voices a desire to do something on her own, Alex objects and gets suspicious. He insists that she "keep the home fires burning" while he's still working as a dentist and for the regular visits from their children.

"My heart isn't in staying anymore," Vida confesses. "I want to talk with Alex, but our conversations just go round and round in circles. It's making me think that the only option I've got is to leave a note and just disappear." She knows that she can be impulsive when pushed to the edge.

"How can I talk with him so I can set myself free to be me while honouring my family?"

What follows is the answer that Vida and I found together to that question.

Know your triggers

A Big Conversation sometimes calls us to deal with our emotions. When someone pushes our buttons and we react with anger, fear or shame, it can really get in the way of us talking together.

Emotional outbursts are like deadly toxins that can kill a conversation in a moment.

When I met Vida it was clear that she was experiencing some highly charged, negative emotions every time she tried to talk with Alex.

"I get so frustrated," she admitted, "that sometimes I just explode."

Vida described Alex as being opinionated, domineering and, at times, arrogant.

"He's very quick to take the moral high ground," Vida observed. "For him, things are either black or white, right or wrong, good or bad. There's no in-between."

Vida also shared that whenever she tried to have a "real conversation" about the future, Alex would get upset and angry and that would stop her from speaking further.

"I can't talk with him, yet I don't want to leave without saying a word. What can I do?"

In our conversations, I noticed that Vida was putting most of her attention on what *Alex* was being, doing and saying. To switch her focus on to what part *she* might be playing in their conversations, I asked Vida to complete the Triggers exercise (see Part III, pages 237–8). I felt that this exercise would help Vida to pinpoint what triggered her when she spoke to Alex and to identify some coping strategies for managing her emotions more effectively. The less reactive she was, the more likely it would be that her next conversation with Alex would be productive.

Doing this exercise enabled Vida to admit to herself the full range of negative emotions that she was experiencing. Naming what she was feeling helped Vida to see how she was allowing herself to get "emotionally hijacked". Vida identified the following emotions and their triggers:

- "I felt depressed when Alex said that he didn't want to spend Christmas with my parents when I've always spent Christmas with his."
- "I felt overwhelmed when Alex told me to go and cut the hedge on his birthday."
- "I felt frustrated when Alex made me come to bed with him when I wasn't ready to sleep."
- "I felt resentful when Alex said he didn't like the way I danced at the party on Saturday night."
- "I felt enraged when Alex dismissed my concerns and said, 'Be happy! Look at everything you've got!'"

We explored which of these emotions felt most out of her control. Vida said it was her anger.

"What causes you to be angry?" I enquired.

Vida was quick to respond. "I think Alex should be listening to my concerns instead of pushing them to one side."

I suggested to Vida that what was really making her angry was her *thought* that Alex should be behaving in a different way.

"Getting over your idea that it's Alex who is making you angry will help you to handle the conversation better," I said. "It's *you* who is making you angry. You have a thought that things should be showing up in a different way than they are. It's your objection that's making you angry, not Alex."

Vida looked thoughtful. "You mean when he pushes my buttons, I don't have to react in the way I do?"

"Exactly," I said. "If you can find a way of slowing down, you'll see that you have a choice about how you respond. Exploding with rage isn't the only option."

We next turned our attention to identifying some coping strategies that Vida could use to respond to Alex in a different way.

Take response-ability

When we start to own our negative emotional reactions, we are making strides toward a Big Conversation. Naming our emotions and seeing them for what they are stops us from being consumed by them. Stepping away from our anger, fear or jealousy enables us to connect the other person in a more respectful way.

To manage our emotions when we're in the midst of a conversation, it helps to work out some strategies in advance. There is often too much going on when we're talking for us to be able to do this emotional management "on the hoof".

When Vida and I reviewed her triggers, we discussed how she could develop an early warning system to enable her to make a different choice instead of losing her temper. By identifying the signals in her body, such as feeling tension in her chest, her face becoming flushed and her temperature rising, Vida could become aware that her anger was starting to take over. Being conscious of the body's intelligence is a simple way of making a real difference to an interaction.

Vida and I then came up with three coping strategies that she could use to regain control of her emotions. These would enable her to *choose* what to say or do next:

- **Take a couple of deep breaths**. Instead of speaking impulsively, she needed to breathe more deeply. This would buy a few crucial seconds for Vida to gather her thoughts.
- **State her disagreement without any drama**. Vida identified that she could say simply and clearly, "I disagree", or "I see things differently from you", without pushing her point further.
- **Declare how she was feeling**. Vera could say a few words to communicate what she was starting

to feel before her emotion reached unmanageable
proportions, such as, "I'm starting to feel irritated".

I suggested to Vida that she try out using the strategies in a
"low-stakes" conversation to see how they worked in practice.
At our next coaching session she reported back that they'd
helped her to keep her cool during a heated conversation with
a neighbour.

"I can see now that this anger is *my* button. I own it." Vida
reflected, before adding, "Learning to manage my emotions
means that I now have more respect for myself."

Taking "response-ability" for her reactions meant that Vida
would be better equipped to talk with Alex when the time for
their Big Conversation came. When we do this work to "clean
up" our emotional responses, there is less static in the air. A conversation can then flow more freely.

Work out what you want

When there is a lot of emotional turmoil in our lives, it is all
too easy for us to become disconnected from who we are and
what we want. Our heartfelt desires get obscured like the sun
covered by a dark cloud. Sometimes we may feel that the only
option is to run away. Moving through the commotion and
reconnecting with ourselves is fundamental to having a life-
changing conversation.

Vida admitted that she was keeping herself busy with charity
events, taking courses and seeing friends as way of distracting
herself from the Big Conversation. When she thought of talking
with Alex about leaving him, she became anxious about how he
would get angry and upset.

"Everything just keeps churning around in my head," Vida
said. "I should have followed my heart and left a year ago. I want
to talk with Alex, but I feel really confused about what to say."

I felt it would help Vida to get in touch with her feelings. Whereas negative *emotions* can disrupt a dialogue, *feelings* can catalyze a conversation. Being aware of the difference between the two helps us to connect with greater respect, both with ourselves and with each other. I shared with Vida these key differences:

- An emotion usually has a clear manifestation in the physical body whereas a feeling is often not rooted in your physicality. A feeling can originate outside the body, as an inner knowingness about something or an intuitive flash that takes you by surprise.

- An emotion, or "energy in motion", is often intense and dramatic. It takes hold of you and, if you have not done your inner work, it can throw you off centre. A feeling, on the other hand, takes you more deeply into yourself. A feeling can last much longer than an emotion, which can erupt and then pass in a few moments.

- Emotions are typically your reaction to something you don't understand. For example, another person intimidates you and you feel scared even if there is no direct threat to your well-being. Feelings, by contrast, are a form of higher understanding. They are the way in which your heart whispers to you. You might "know", for example, that the person you've just met is going to play a significant role in your life.

Because they are subtle, feelings can be difficult to discover and sometimes even more tricky to acknowledge. To connect with what we feel, we need to put distractions to one side. It is in this silence that our heart speaks its secrets to us. I suggested to

Vida that she set aside half an hour to write her responses to the following three questions:

- What don't I want?
- What do I want?
- What's stopping me from going after this?

Vida returned to our next coaching session saying that she'd struggled to answer these questions. I could feel her heaviness hanging like the air before a storm. Vida said she'd tried to answer the questions, but nothing had come.

Sensing her distress, I said, "You have a right to your joy, Vida. Husband or no husband, career or no career."

Vida looked at me and some tears fell slowly, silently down her cheeks. During the rest of our session little else was said. We sat side by side, her hand in mine, as she breathed her way through the birth pangs of her new existence.

A few coaching sessions later, I could see a real shift in Vida. Her eyes were bright, her cheeks were pink and her voice was strong. She shared with me that she'd gone for a long walk the day before and, on her return, had done some journaling. She had identified what she *didn't* want:

- "To live a meaningless life that's been decided *for* me rather than *by* me."
- "To feel chained to commitments not of my own choosing."

Vida was then able to articulate what she *did* want:

- "To be free to live and work with my passion for gardening."
- "To follow my path and become the person I really am."

Vida and I then explored what was stopping her from moving forward.

"It's very hard to go after 30 years of being married," Vida reflected. "I've wanted to not betray Alex, but now I can see that I'm betraying myself by staying. I need to find a way to talk to him so that I can go with my integrity intact, rather than just walking out.

"I don't want to be talked into staying. I feel I've been tethered for years now and it's time for me to set myself free."

Now that Vida was feeling centred, she was ready to reach out to Alex in a more balanced way. Once we are connected with our own heart, the conversation with another person can run more freely.

Change your tune

Getting centred can make all the difference to a Big Conversation. In some cases, it might mean that we stay and talk rather than just pack our bags and leave.

"I get stuck because I think that what I want is too hurtful to say," Vida shared. "So I end up obsessing about it instead."

A Big Conversation often calls on us to "change our tune" and relate to another person in a different way. I shared with Vida that I've found there are four "languages of conversation", each of which creates a different kind of connection (see Figure 7).

Ideally, we would be able to express ourselves in all four languages at any given moment. In reality, many of us don't have this capacity and, as a result, a Big Conversation can be cut short. Developing our awareness of the four languages makes connecting with someone else more possible.

To help Vida prepare for talking with Alex, I suggested she complete the Tune in exercise (see Part III, pages 239–41). This would help her to identify which of the four languages

Figure 7 – The four languages of conversation	
Language of the head	**Language of the heart**
Connecting with others through:	Connecting with others through:
• Sharing our thinking and opinions • Finding meaning in what's said • Bringing together different ideas • Understanding the key issues	• Expressing our feelings • Providing a sense of warmth • Being willing to open up • Showing we care about others
Language of the hands	**Language of the horizon**
Connecting with others through:	Connecting with others through:
• Providing practical suggestions • Taking care of the details • Focusing on what will get done • Considering the *now*	• Using our imagination • Looking at the bigger picture • Considering future possibilities • Noticing patterns and intuitions

she typically used and which she was most likely to overlook, enabling Vida to reach out to Alex in a new way.

Vida found that her strongest preference was to use the language of the **head.** She was most at ease when sharing her thinking, opinions and ideas. This tendency also meant that at times she could "overthink" what she wanted to say, rather than speak it out loud. At other times Vida would use the language of the **hands**. She liked to talk about the practicalities of a situation and what was happening here and now.

The language Vida said she was least likely to use was that of the **heart.** She tended to shy away from expressing her feelings, from showing warmth and from voicing her concerns for the other person. "Alex has told me that he sometimes finds me critical and a bit hard," Vida told me.

In the absence of the language of the heart, a Big Conversation might feel cold, calculated and incomplete. Unless we speak from the heart, it is hard to create the sense of connection that is needed.

Vida said that, for her, speaking from the heart felt very challenging. "I'm scared of speaking about how I feel, because what I want to say may be too painful for Alex to hear." She paused. "I'm struggling to break out of this pattern."

I could understand Vida's concern about not wanting to hurt Alex. I also felt, however, that if she *could* find a way to speak from her heart, she would at least stand in integrity with him.

"What if how the message is sent is more important than how it is received?" I asked. "You aren't responsible for how Alex feels or how he responds. All you can do is to say what you need to say with as much care as possible."

Vida was very thoughtful for the rest of our session. We explored how she could connect with Alex in a more heartfelt way by:

- **Voicing how she was feeling**. This would help her to open up the conversation, for example by saying, "I've been feeling sad about how we seem to have drifted apart over the years" and "I can't go on feeling so unfulfilled in my life."
- **Sharing her concerns about the impact on Alex**. This would help to create some empathy, for example by saying, "It would be good to talk about what support you'd need if you stayed living in this house on your own."
- **Allowing Alex to express himself**. Even if his

response made her feel uncomfortable, Vida could acknowledge how Alex might be feeling, for example by saying, "I guess this is making you feel sad, too. Are you OK to keep on talking?"

Vida observed, "I'm realizing that I haven't really told Alex how I feel. I don't normally speak from my heart, but now I've got an idea of what to say, I think I can."

I shared with Vida that, in my experience, some heartfelt words are often able to build a bridge to another person when all else fails.

Speak their language

One of the challenges, and joys, of conversation is that our connection with each person is unique. We are all wired in our own distinct way. There are, however, some patterns in how we talk together that can help us to navigate a Big Conversation. If we are sensitive to the *other person's* preferences regarding the four different languages of conversation, we will be able to speak to them in a way that they understand.

Having shared with me her perception that she and Alex "talked different languages", Vida identified that his major preference was for the future focused language of the **horizon**. This meant that at times Vida found conversations with him overwhelming as she preferred to keep focused on practicalities, using the language of the **hands**.

Given Alex's preference for talking in terms of the bigger picture, Vida and I discussed how she could "join" Alex there. I asked her to consider a number of possible future scenarios for them as a couple. I felt that it could help Alex if Vida talked through how each of these scenarios made her feel, by showing that she had thought through the different options carefully:

- **Staying at home** – Continuing to live under the same roof, doing some charity work together and spending some of the winter abroad. "This makes me feel depressed, although less selfish with regards to Alex and the children," said Vida.
- **Staying in the UK** – separating from Alex, moving into a place of her own and getting a job. "I feel heavy hearted about this future," noted Vida, "although less guilty about moving far away from the children."
- **Working abroad** – separating from Alex, going to a warmer climate and getting a job to support herself financially. "This makes me feel scared and excited," Vida said. "And I know it's where my heart is."

"It's been very helpful to think about the different scenarios," Vida reflected. "I don't usually talk in these terms, but then this isn't the usual conversation."

By finding a way to frame what she had to say in terms that Alex could relate to, Vida was one step closer to having the Big Conversation.

Ride the resistance

One of the reasons why we get so nervous about having a Big Conversation is that we're not in control of how it unfolds. We may have done our work to ground ourselves and speak the language of the other person, but what if they become angry, get upset or shut down? Given that a Big Conversation can change our own life *and* the lives of those around us, it is likely to create disturbance.

A typical response when we meet resistance is either to back off or to meet it head on. However, meeting negativity with more negativity creates a "texture" to the interaction that is not conducive to talking together.

Vida reflected that she and Alex were locked into a pattern of blaming each other and couldn't seem to shift out of it.

"There's a lot of finger pointing that goes on," Vida observed. "We're quite critical and judgmental with each other."

I suggested that Vida complete the Texture exercise (see Part III, pages 244–6), to look at whether she was broadcasting "positive" or "negative" energy when she spoke to Alex:

- **Positive energy** comes from expressing qualities such as appreciation, interest and curiosity.
- **Negative energy** comes from being contemptuous, disdainful and disapproving.

Vida and I reviewed the balance of positive and negative energy and found that what she typically said to Alex was significantly biased toward the negative. As this narrows the possibility of having a life-changing conversation, I was keen to help Vida to shift her tone.

I asked Vida to identify some positive messages she could give Alex. I suggested that she tell me what she genuinely *appreciated* about her husband, their relationship and the current situation. Figure 8 on page 134 shows what she came up with.

This is not about sucking up to the other person or insincerely "oiling the wheels". It is about shifting the tone of the conversation. When the air becomes clogged with criticism, cynicism and contempt, no real conversation is possible. Neutralizing negativity with some genuine, heartfelt words of appreciation makes a conversation possible across the widest chasm.

Vida and I then explored the most hurtful, difficult and challenging things Alex might say *to her* as their Big Conversation unfolded. Anticipating the other person's objections makes us more likely to be able to deal with them. I asked Vida to identify the kindest thing she could say in response. Figure 8.1 on page 135 shows what she wrote down.

Figure 8 – Shifting the tone of Vida's conversation	
Negativity: What Vida typically said	**Positivity:** What Vida *could* say
• Stop being so controlling!" • "I find you really opinionated." • "You're always on my case about spending too much time on the computer." • "Leave me alone!" • "I hate it when you tell me what to do."	• "You've been a great provider for me and the family for over 20 years." • "You're a very good father and have always been there for the kids." • "I appreciate the changes you've made over the last year, such as buying me flowers and saying kind things." • "You're very good at getting things done." • "I'm finding the current situation hard, but it's made me more aware of this deep longing I feel inside for something else." • "I'd like us to find a way of talking together because I really care about you and the kids and about what happens to us all."

Figure 8.1 – Shifting the tone of Vida's conversation	
What Alex might say to Vida	**What Vida could say in response**
"I can't cope."	"I'm sorry that what I say makes you feel that way, but it doesn't change how I feel."
"It's not a good idea for you to leave. It will make you vulnerable."	"I understand that this is upsetting for you, but I have to do it. I need to go and be who I am."
"You need to stay and be a supportive wife because I still have my job to do. I have always supported you financially. Why won't you support me?"	"It's better that I go and come back willingly, if that happens. Otherwise, I'll only stay grudgingly and we won't stand a chance of ever being happy together."

"This is tough stuff," Vida said as she reviewed her potential responses. "But I do feel more confident now about having the Big Conversation."

Vida steadied herself to meet Alex's resistance with equanimity instead of animosity. Harsh words can sever not only a conversation but a relationship for ever. Finding a way within ourselves to talk with compassion can make all the difference in the world.

Listen with your heart

Each conversation has its own rhythm. Its pulse comes from speaking authentically and listening with an open heart to what the other person has to say. Ultimately, a Big Conversation has less to do with anything we *achieve* and more to do with what we *receive*. What is beautiful in life arises out of mutuality rather than from "me, me, me".

Listening to someone else can be demanding. At times we may find our eyes glazing over as we "zone out". The things the other person says may hurt us. However, when we are committed to being real, we no longer mind the hurt so much. We realize that there is part of us that is above being hurt when we're called a betrayer, accused of lying and judged as selfish. It might take every fibre in our being to stay and listen, but it is this deep receptivity that turns around a stuck situation.

In a Big Conversation we need to be aware of ourselves so that we notice when we start to switch off. It helps to be sensitive to the other person, alert to the flickers of anger, disgust or shame that flash across their face. When Vida and I talked through how she could keep her heart open to Alex during their Big Conversation, we found three things to help her:

- **Sitting still instead of moving about**. Vida often felt restless when she talked with Alex and would pace up and down. Making a conscious decision to calm down physically would help her to quieten herself mentally.

- **Breathing into the heart**. Vida practised taking a few deep breaths to expand her heart space. As she felt her shoulders drop and her jaw unclench, she became calmer and more centred.

- **Maintaining eye contact**. Vida reflected that she often looked away when Alex got angry or upset. She decided to soften her gaze and keep looking at him as a way of showing respect and staying connected.

"I'm starting to feel OK about talking with Alex," Vida said after we'd talked through how she could keep connected as they conversed.

When I first met Vida, she had been about to run away, but now she was ready to reach out. She was embracing what she had been putting off for so long. She was prepared to have the Big Conversation.

From the heart

The thought of picking the right moment to talk with Alex filled Vida with anxiety.

"I've got to stop shilly-shallying around," she said, as she reminded herself of all the preparation she'd done.

Vida waited for a weekend when the children weren't visiting, when she and Alex could be alone. Her first thought was to ask Alex to go for walk, but she remembered the importance of eye contact so they could connect properly. She decided that they needed to sit facing each other, even though that felt more scary.

On the Saturday afternoon, after taking some time to get centred by going for a short walk by herself, Vida found Alex in his study and asked if they could talk. As she sat down, she felt full of trepidation – and a little excited.

"We need to talk," Vida began. "I've been feeling very unsettled and sad for a while now."

Vida made sure that she looked Alex straight in the eye and spoke as gently as she could. A little while later she shared with him the truth of her heart.

"I love you, but I'm not in love with you," she said. "I value your friendship but no longer feel a passionate connection with you."

Vida kept quiet as she let Alex absorb her words. After a long pause he spoke.

"But this is what happens after 20 years of marriage," he replied. "You and I have moved into a mature relationship."

As the conversation progressed, Alex got upset and Vida did her best to stay as calm as she could. She acknowledged how painful the conversation must be for him. Vida felt relieved that she'd anticipated Alex's resistance and had some words to say in response. When it felt appropriate, she thanked him for all the good times they'd shared and said what a great father he'd been.

Taking a deep breath, Vida repeated that she wanted to release herself from what she saw as an outdated commitment. She listened to Alex's objections without interrupting him, getting angry or leaving the room.

As Alex calmed down, he admitted to Vida that he, too, had made mistakes in their marriage. When he said he would make some changes, Vida made it clear that she wanted to create a new life for herself. She offered to be the first to tell the children, no longer afraid of having the conversation with them. As they brought their own conversation to a close, Alex agreed to talk more about how they could separate, saying that he'd prefer them to do so slowly and carefully.

With an unknown path stretching out ahead, Vida felt sadness but also relief and an immeasurable joy that she had taken the first step toward freedom. She had had her Big Conversation.

Summary

When we connect wholeheartedly with another person, a Big Conversation can happen. Talking together can be the start of a whole new adventure if we reach out with respect. To help make this happen:

1. **Know your triggers**. Raise your awareness of what pushes your buttons. Name the troublesome emotions that get you "triggered". This will help you to create a six-second pause and to be more relaxed and less reactive.

2. **Take "response-ability"**. Identify some coping strategies for managing difficult emotions such as anger, fear or

jealousy. Practise using these strategies in low-stake conversations to build your ability to stay centred.

3. **Work out what you want.** Get in touch with your feelings. Take some time to go within. Know what you *do* want as well as what you don't want. Ask yourself what's stopping you from moving forward and how you can overcome any obstacles.

4. **Change your tune.** Be aware of which of the four languages of conversation you are most likely to use and which ones you overlook. Explore ways of integrating the missing languages into your conversation.

5. **Speak their language.** Express yourself in ways the other person will understand. Identify which of the four languages they are most likely to respond to and use this in your communication.

6. **Ride the resistance.** Anticipate the resistance you are likely to meet. Neutralize negativity with appreciation, curiosity and empathy. Identify in advance the most challenging things the other person might say and think about how you will respond.

7. **Listen with your heart.** Develop your receptivity. Notice when you start to zone out and make sure you re-engage. Focus on what the other person has to say by keeping still, maintaining eye contact and breathing into your heart.

Getting over emotional hijack

Emotional outbursts, such as exploding with rage, can be very damaging. They take place in an instant, but their impact can last a long time. As a result of what we said or did in the heat of the moment, the other person might retaliate or avoid talking to us. Learning to manage our emotions makes a real difference to our conversations and relationships.

Neuroscientific research shows that emotions are chemical reactions that last just six seconds in the body. If we experience them for longer, it is only because we are choosing to. For example, when we feel threatened, our "fight-or-flight" response kicks in and floods our body with stress hormones.

Re-engaging our thinking brain (neocortex) after it has been "hijacked" by our emotional brain (amygdala) is a key conversational skill. As Joshua Freedman points out in his 2007 book, *At the Heart of Leadership*, to avoid a shouting match or stony silence, we need to create a six-second pause to help us to keep our cool and our conversation on track. Scientific research shows three things help:

1. **Noticing where in your body you feel the emotion**. Is the frustration or anxiety in your chest, your stomach or somewhere else?

2. **Naming the emotion**. Are you feeling angry, impatient or fearful? Identifying and labelling the specific emotion helps it to subside.

3. **Buying yourself some time**. Take a couple of deep breaths. Count to 10. Ask to pause the conversation. Go for a walk. Get a drink of water.

These three steps generate a "moment of choice". Activate your thinking by asking yourself, "Whation in a positive way?" Getting over an emotional hijack can transfat's the best response I can make here?" "What's the most appropriate thing to say?" "How can I contribute to this converssorm how we talk together.

CHAPTER 8

Shift 5 – Speak your truth

"You shall know the truth, and the truth shall set you free."

John 8:32

A Big Conversation calls on us to speak our truth. This often makes us feel uncomfortable. Because we're afraid to rock the boat, cause unpleasantness or damage a relationship, we avoid talking about what matters most. However, when we realize that the fastest way to heal a hurt or to make our life "take off" is to say what's true, a conversation becomes not only possible but inspirational.

Failing to speak our truth is a major source of stress in our lives. When we wear a mask rather than express ourselves authentically, we are trapped into acting out a role. Instead of being who we really are, we become a counterfeit version of ourselves. This makes us feel drained, down and desperate.

Getting our lives back on track through an honest conversation is a twofold process. The first step is to tell the truth to ourselves. This involves becoming aware of feelings and needs that we might find hard to acknowledge. Our truth arises out of all that is within us. Uncovering our truth is vital, life-changing work.

The second step is to tell our truth to another person. Even when there are hard things to say, expressing ourselves does not have to be destructive. Speaking the truth does not in itself damage a relationship. What is essential is *how* we speak our truth. A Big Conversation stands or falls by the degree to which we are able to give voice to our observations, thoughts and feelings clearly, compassionately and completely.

To set ourselves free to live the life we choose sometimes demands a Big Conversation. Whether it's with our boss, our partner or a member of our family, talking transparently can be tough. Having some tools to help us through the truth process can make all the difference. Equipping you to stand in your truth is what this chapter is all about.

Talk it out

You've been working hard for years without feeling fulfilled. You've settled for making a living rather than having a life. You're fed up with your job and how your boss is treating you, but you're afraid to rock the boat as jobs are hard to come by in the present economic climate. You have a family to consider and provide for. You want to talk with your boss but know that the Big Conversation may result in your resignation. Before you go out on a limb and speak your truth, you need to be sure it's the right thing to do. Finding a way to talk without compromising who you are or what you want is becoming urgent. You can't bear the feeling that life is passing you by any longer.

Tim knows just what this scenario feels like.

Tim is a conscientious, successful graphic designer in his mid-thirties. He started his career in his early twenties in a large design consultancy in London, where he "worked like crazy". Seven years ago he decided he wanted a more balanced life and moved to the Cotswolds to take up a post in a small design business. Although he's always put in the hours, Tim strongly believes that, "there's more to life than working". The recent death of his father has brought home to him how important it is to enjoy a meaningful and fulfilled life.

Two years ago the design business where Tim works rebranded itself. Tim's workload increased significantly and now he often leaves the office after 7pm. A keen marathon runner who likes to train in the evenings, he resents the fact that his physical fitness is suffering as a result of the long working day with an hour's commute either side. He's noticed that he's put on weight and that his thick, wavy hair is now more grey than blonde. His wife says that he's lost the twinkle in his eye that attracted her when they first met. She wants Tim to spend more time with her and their baby son who is now six months old.

Tim likes to do his best for his boss, Alison, who sees Tim as her deputy. Alison is the owner of the business and now employs six graphic designers. She has a strong work ethic and has just had a second child. Alison's husband, with whom Tim has become good friends, admits, over a drink, that Alison is finding it challenging to run the business while looking after a young family. Moreover, morale has been dropping in recent months. Tim puts this down to Alison's expectation that the staff work unpaid overtime and also to her reneging on a promise to give them an additional day off over Christmas in return for all their hard work. After heavy snow shut the office, Alison withdrew the extra day's holiday, messing up plans with families and friends.

As part of the rebrand, Alison made Tim a director of the company. At first Tim was delighted that his hard work and diligent approach had been recognized. When the new business cards were handed out, Tim felt a surge of pride to see "Design Director" next to his name. However, the thrill gradually wore off. There was no financial reward, the other graphic designers carried on reporting to Alison and Tim wasn't consulted on the new strategy for growing the business.

"When I hand out my business card to clients," Tim says, "I feel like a fraud." It seems that the directorship is in name only. He feels let down, demotivated and undervalued. He's recently found himself thinking about retraining to be a sports massage therapist, a dream he's had since his teenage years.

Tim knows that he's been avoiding talking to Alison. "It makes me anxious just thinking about it," he confesses. His wife, Liz, is fed up with him moaning and groaning about the situation yet taking no action. She complains that Tim's vociferous with her but silent with Alison. When Tim and Liz had yet another argument over Christmas about him not speaking out, Tim decided to get in touch with me for some coaching.

"The conversation with Alison is on my mind all the time. I feel like a real wimp but I don't know what to say or how to bring it up."

Having a young family to support, Tim was keen not to resign in anger. "How can I speak my truth without damaging the relationship? I don't want to burn my bridges workwise," Tim told me. What follows is the answer we worked through step by step.

Address the undiscussables

A Big Conversation starts with us telling the truth to ourselves. This includes being honest with ourselves about the conversations we've been avoiding. Somewhat paradoxically, raising our own awareness of which issues are currently off-limits helps to generate energy for talking. Taking a good look at the "undiscussables" brings a Big Conversation out of the closet and onto the table.

If left unaddressed, difficult or sensitive topics don't go away. They fester. They make their presence felt like a bad smell. We sense them hanging in the air. Recognizing this unease is important. The way forward is not to try to eliminate our discomfort, but to accept that there will be some disturbance as things get aired. There are, however, things we can do to move more easily through the perturbation.

To get us started, I asked Tim to complete the Elephants exercise (see Part III, pages 247–9, and Figure 9, page 146). Identifying the "elephants in the room" – those topics that everyone knows are there but no one wants to talk about – can reveal possible ways to approach the conversation. Turning the undiscussables into discussables calls for some careful reflection.

Tim identified a number of topics he considered taboo to discuss with Alison. We made a distinction between those he would be comfortable discussing and those he wouldn't be. As the truth is often to be found in what's undiscussable and uncomfortable, this is where Tim and I focused our attention. We took each of the topics in turn and explored the question "What would it take to make this discussable, even with some discomfort?".

As we took a good look at each of the undiscussables, Tim's reticence about talking with Alison started to shift. He reflected that he had a strong value of fairness, which he felt had been violated by Alison's aggressive push to work long hours. When Tim saw that his silence wasn't congruent with his belief in equitable treatment, not only for himself but also for others, he felt more committed to having a conversation about it.

However, the big "ah-ha" came a little later. "I can see now that I don't have to try to solve everything in a single conversation," Tim suddenly said. "That makes it feel a lot less daunting."

Recognizing his ability to raise the issues one at a time in a sequence of conversations helped Tim to let go of his need to keep the peace at all costs. He was one step closer to having the Big Conversation with Alison.

Do a reality check

As we have seen, a Big Conversation begins with us telling the truth to ourselves. But that simple sentence – so easy to write – implies a significant amount of work if we are make our truth an effective force to help us.

Before we can communicate fully with another person, we need to know our truth. Finding our truth is not about finding the Truth. Philosophers and theologians have spent centuries thinking and writing about universal Truth. What we are dealing with here is an individual's truth, which is

Figure 9 – Tim's elephants		
	Discussable	Undiscussable
Comfortable	Design ideas for clients Client relationships	How to grow the company Improving my performance My frustration with my role as director
Uncomfortable	Asking for time off Which items count as company expenses	Alison's expectations about working hours That I'm thinking of a possible career change

their perception of what's appropriate and life-affirming right here, right now. In conversation there are no absolute truths, just different perceptions. The clearer we are about how we view a situation, the better able we will be to tell our truth to someone else.

Our truth emerges from our data, which fills our personal databank. There are three different elements to this databank: our observations, our thoughts and our feelings. Our truth becomes clouded when we overlook any one of these elements. Ignoring that we're feeling frustrated, for example, distorts our view of the situation. We might try to convince ourselves that everything's fine, while our energy drains away and we lose our verve. When we suppress our feelings, it stops a Big Conversation in its tracks.

To get to our truth, it helps to separate out our observations, thoughts and feelings, just as crude oil is distilled into a number of different substances. We can better distil our truth by distinguishing between what we observe, what we think and what we feel.

When I first met Tim, he wasn't sure what he made of his work situation. To help Tim to get to his truth, I asked him to create a "truth inventory" (see Figure 10, page 148). He started by identifying his **observations**. These are facts about the current reality that could be objectively recorded. Our observations are not about stating what we *imagine* is the case; they are about observing "what's so". Writing down our observations is a useful reality check.

Next, I asked Tim to write down his **thoughts**. Whereas our observations are the "raw data", this is the "analyzed data". Ultimately our thoughts are simply mental constructs – ideas that we make up. They include our judgments, interpretations and evaluations. Distinguishing our thoughts from our observations helps to expose any fictions we're telling ourselves.

I challenged Tim that the following were his opinions rather than objective observations:

- "I'm not up to the role of director."
- "I don't know where I stand."
- "I think Alison's changed her mind about wanting me to be a director."

When Tim accepted that these were his own mental constructs rather than statements of "what's so", his perspective started to shift.

"Maybe it's all in my head that I'm no good at being a director," Tim reflected. "I've not actually had a performance appraisal for two years. I've begun to doubt myself, but maybe that's my view rather than Alison's."

Figure 10 – Tim's truth inventory	
Observations	Thoughts
Made Design Director two years ago.	I'm not up to the role of director.
No salary increase as a director.	I don't know where I stand.
No performance appraisal for the last two years.	I think Alison's changed her mind about wanting me to be a director.
Overseeing client relationships has increased my workload.	I'm a perfectionist and the rest of the team are not as conscientious as I am.
Often work after 7pm whereas contracted hours are to 5.30pm.	I've played a big part in the success of this company.

When we switch from making judgments to sharing observations, we become less locked into our own narrow view of what's happening. We get closer to knowing our truth. Difficulties in communication sometimes stem from confusing what we think is the case with "what's so". Making the distinction helps to keep communication channels clear when the time to talk comes.

Listen to your feelings

The largest part of surfacing our truth is listening to our **feelings**. This is the data that we are most likely to overlook, but it is also the most informative. What is true for us often lies beyond the reach of our conscious mind. It rises up from a deeper place where we feel things without always knowing why. Getting back in touch with our senses is crucial if we are to speak our truth.

Admitting to ourselves how we're feeling sounds simple but is not easy. We often mistake our thoughts for feelings. Being clear about what we're feeling as well as thinking helps us to know our truth more fully. When we know what's true for us, we will be able to share it more easily with another person.

I asked Tim to write down all the different feelings he was experiencing about his work situation. When he shared his notes with me, I noticed that some weren't really feelings at all. They *looked* like feelings, but they were opinions masquerading as feelings. For example:

- "I feel that I'm underappreciated by Alison."
- "I feel like a failure."

These are Tim's judgments about the situation rather than expressions of what he's actually feeling. As Marshall Rosenberg points out in *Non-violent Communication* (2003), when "I feel" is followed by words such as "that" or "like", it's a thought not a feeling.

Tim also made the following statements:

- "I feel Alison's not being fair to me."
- "I feel it's pointless to say anything."

Similarly, this is Tim assessing the situation rather than expressing what he's feeling. Pronouns such as "she" or "it" after "I feel" are a good indicator that we're giving voice to an opinion. Just because a statement begins with "I feel …", it does not mean that it describes a true feeling.

To help Tim uncover his actual feelings, I suggested he complete the Wheel exercise (see Part III, pages 250–51). The wheel in this exercise is a map we can use to pinpoint how we are feeling. There are many nuances to what goes on inside us and it helps to have clarity, first, about which of the six core feelings we are experiencing. We might be feeling:

- Happy
- Sad
- Angry
- Envious
- Ashamed
- Fearful

Once we are clear about the broad emotional territory we are in, we can then move to a more detailed description. There are many different shades to what we feel and we can experience more than one feeling at a time.

Being precise about our feelings facilitates a conversation. Saying "I'm furious about …", for example, conveys a very different message to "I'm cross about …". The more specific we can be about what we're feeling, the more powerful our truth telling will be.

Using the map in the Wheel exercise, Tim realized that he was feeling sad, angry and fearful. Taking each of these feelings in turn, he identified more specifically that:

- "I'm feeling frustrated at the relentless pace at which Alison wants me to work."
- "I'm disappointed that the Design Director role now seems meaningless."
- "I'm anxious about my future career and providing for my young family."

"It's a relief to know how I'm feeling," Tim said. "I had no idea that all those feelings were bubbling away under the surface." Our feelings are often the missing piece of the puzzle when we're telling the truth to ourselves about ourselves. This self-honesty is pivotal to a Big Conversation.

Have a R.A.N.T.

Once we've told the truth to ourselves about ourselves, it's time to tell the truth to ourselves about the other person. Expressing ourselves offline before the Big Conversation comes online helps raise our awareness about what we *actually* need to say. If we do this work beforehand, we are less likely to get derailed during the conversation and say things that we might regret later.

Expressing ourselves fully, truthfully and responsibly is an art. Sometimes, the moment we say something aloud, it no longer feels true. When we shout at someone, for example, and release the suppressed anger, the rage we were feeling may go away. Underneath the heat there may even be some positive feelings that we weren't aware of before. Being honest with ourselves about how we're feeling about another person allows for the possibility that, as we express ourselves, our truth changes.

To help Tim tell the truth to himself about Alison, I encouraged him to complete the R.A.N.T. exercise (see Part III, pages 252–3). Tim expressed what he **R**esented, **A**ppreciated and

Needed in relation to Alison. Once he'd got clarity about these things, it would be easier for him to distil his Truth.

Tim wrote down what he was feeling about Alison as if he were speaking directly to her. He used the phrases "I resent you for ...", "I appreciate you for ..." and "I need you to ...", in order to bring a directness, honesty and immediacy that might not surface otherwise.

Giving voice to how we're feeling in the present tense and with specific details means that "the moment's truth is spoken in its entirety", as Brad Blanton writes in *Radical Honesty* (2003). While Brad Blanton recommends voicing these statements person to person, my suggestion is to write them down, say them out loud and see which of them still ring true. Expressing our resentments, appreciations and needs to ourselves first helps to reduce the risk that we offend the other person while we work out what our truth really is.

To begin with, Tim struggled to articulate why he resented Alison. The frustration was there, in his tight-set mouth and the pinched look on his face, but Tim couldn't get a handle on it. It can be tricky to acknowledge how we're feeling when we're used to repressing our emotions. I suggested that he start by getting in touch with what he was feeling in his body. "There's a tightness in my throat," Tim observed. "And some tension in my jaw."

I asked Tim to bring to mind some incidents involving Alison that he connected with this feeling of contraction in his body. He spoke of a time when Alison had gone on holiday, leaving another colleague to complete a pitch for some new work. Tim said that he and Alison both knew this designer was not capable of completing the proposal to the required standard and that Tim would end up doing the work himself.

"Alison assumed I'd take care of it," Tim vented. "She takes advantage of my conscientiousness. She knows I'll put myself out and make sure things are done right."

We went on to explore other incidents in which Tim felt resentful about how he'd been treated by Alison. I encouraged him to be specific about what made him feel bitter.

We then turned our attention to what Tim appreciated about Alison. He looked thoughtful. "Now I've got all that other stuff off my chest," Tim said, "I can think of several things I'm grateful for."

Finally we looked at what Tim needed from Alison. Often, when we feel resentful, it's because we have unmet needs. Surfacing these needs can be challenging.

"Most of us have never been taught to think in terms of our needs," Marshall Rosenberg writes in *Nonviolent Communication*. However, he goes on to observe that "From the moment people begin talking about what they need rather than what's wrong with one another, the possibility of finding ways to meet everyone's needs is greatly increased."

Tim took his time to think about his unmet needs. He found it helpful to go back to his resentments and to dig underneath these. "I've not thought in terms of my needs before," Tim said. "My focus has always been on what Alison was doing wrong. Now I can see that I'm partly responsible for the situation because I've had all these needs that I've not spoken about." The resentments, appreciations and needs Tim identified are given in Figure 11 on page 154.

Acknowledging our unmet needs helps to shift how we're feeling. Our resentment might not disappear, but it does become more manageable. And once we put our feelings in perspective, we can see if our truth has changed.

The final part of the R.A.N.T. exercise involves reading aloud the written statements. When we express our resentments, appreciations and needs out loud, we can learn what still strikes a chord. When Tim voiced his statements, he found that some of them still resonated while others no longer had the "ring of truth". Tim shared with me that when he said aloud, "I resent you for not buying the first round when the team goes out for a drink," he could sense the pettiness of it. While it was still true for him, it wasn't at the heart of the matter.

"My truth," Tim concluded, "is that I'm fed up with working such long hours. I'm frustrated with Alison taking advantage of my conscientiousness and I'm resenting the impact on my personal life. *That's* the nut to crack in all this.

Figure 11 – Tim's R.A.N.T.		
I Resent you for ...	**I Appreciate you for ...**	**I Need you to ...**
• Taking advantage of my conscientiousness and willingness to stay late. • Assuming that I'll complete the pitch when you're away. • Being vague with me about what the Design Director role really means. • Not taking the time to give me proper feedback about my performance. • Not buying the first round when the team goes out for a drink.	• Making me feel part of the business by inviting me to pitch to new clients. • Valuing my input when you ask me to review the CVs for new recruits. • Sharing your passion about design and all the energy you put in.	• Be realistic about how long the work will take when you quote for jobs. • Listen to me and take my input into account when making decisions. • Clarify what my responsibilities are as Design Director. • Give me a formal appraisal and feedback every six months.
My Truth about this situation is ...		
I'm fed up with working such long hours. I'm frustrated with Alison taking advantage of my conscientiousness and I'm resenting the impact on my personal life. I need to make a change and it's up to me to make it happen.		

"I can also see that I need to make a change and it's up to me to make it happen."

Where there had been confusion, there was now clarity. Where there had been resentment, there was now some resolution. Where there had been inertia, there was now impetus. By telling the truth to himself, Tim was another step closer to having the Big Conversation with Alison.

Express yourself – often

Once we know our truth, the next step is to tell it to the other person. This means speaking the truth of our observations, feelings, thoughts and needs. A Big Conversation happens only when we express what we are really experiencing.

Tim shared with me that he was feeling anxious about talking with Alison. Because she'd recently had a second child, he had been reluctant to have the Big Conversation for fear of upsetting her.

"I've left it for so long," he told me, "I've been unable to say anything at all."

However, Tim had a change of heart after a very challenging week. He stayed at the office until 10pm two nights in a row to complete some visuals for a new client, as one of the senior designers had gone on paternity leave. As this colleague wasn't due back for another week, Tim could see his own days getting longer and longer.

Returning to the realization that he could raise the issues one conversation at a time, I asked Tim what his top priority was. "It's not that 'Design Director' is only a title or the lack of a salary increase that gets me," Tim said. "It's the relentless pressure with the long days and ever-increasing workload. I feel I don't have a life anymore."

He paused and asked, "But because I haven't raised the issue before, how can I speak my truth without making a mess of the conversation and ruining the relationship with Alison?"

Building on the work we'd done so far, I suggested to Tim that he kept in mind a simple acronym. In my own Big Conversations, a four-letter *aide-memoire* had become a great ally in keeping me on track when I needed to speak my truth.

"Remember to express yourself OFT'N," I said to Tim. I then explained what each of these letters stood for:

- **O is for observations** Begin by sharing your perception of "what's so". Leave to one side your judgments, opinions and assertions. Focus on the facts. Start with what you can both agree is the reality of the situation.

- **F is for feelings**. Share what you're experiencing. Express your happiness, sadness, anger, envy, shame, fear or other emotion using simple "I" statements, such as "I'm frustrated." Avoid false "I feel"s such as "I feel that you're not being fair."

- **T is for thinking**. Reveal how you perceive the situation. Speak of "what's working" and "what's not working". Avoid talking in terms of "right" and "wrong". Own what you say, as in "I think what's not working here is …".

- **N is for needs**. Request what you need. Take responsibility for what you want to be different. Your need could be for acknowledgement, appreciation or a more practical change. State your need without making heavy work of it.

"I think I'll be able to remember to express myself OFT'N," Tim said, making some notes. "Having a structure will make me more focused and less emotional."

I encouraged Tim to write down the actual words he would say, starting with his observations.

"Once you've got some of the actual words you'd use, a Big Conversation becomes much more manageable," I shared, as I left him to work out the details of how he could express himself OFT'N.

Walk your talk

At our next session, Tim began by saying how useful he'd found the OFT'N principle.

"I've been thinking about it a lot," he shared. "Thank you. I'll be able to speak my truth using it. This feels like a breakthrough."

Tim declared that he had a question for me. "Why isn't it OFTEN? What's happened to the 'E'?"

I responded that I'd made a conscious decision to remove this letter. "In my mind," I said, "the 'E' stands for 'expectations', which can ruin a conversation. If we expect that we'll damage the relationship, it stops us from speaking out.

"In my experience," I continued, "when I've expressed myself openly, honestly and respectfully, it's hardly ever been destructive. If it has been, it's because the other person chose to experience my truth in a negative way and there is little I could have done to avoid that.

"What I've learned the hard way is that when I chose to *hide* my truth, it's *always* been damaging to a relationship."

Tim looked thoughtful. "So what you're saying", he checked, "is that I should speak my truth as best I can instead of hesitating and expecting that I'll ruin the relationship?"

"That's it," I confirmed. "Ultimately, you can only be responsible for what you say. If you set aside your expectations about the mess you'll make, you'll express yourself more freely."

I added that there was one more important aspect to truth telling. "Ultimately, it's not *what* you say, it's *how* you say it that really matters," I said. "It's *who you are*, not the words you speak, that sends the strongest message.

"If you speak arrogantly, the other person is likely to turn away. If you speak harshly, the other person is likely to stop listening. If you speak unkindly, the other person is likely to withdraw. A conversation is a two-way exchange in which both parties are engaged. If the other person backs off, it's no longer a conversation."

In a Big Conversation, therefore, it is essential that we speak our truth in such a way that the other person keeps on conversing with us. Returning to OFT'N, I shared with Tim which tones I'd learned were the most effective for:

- **Observations** – when describing "what's so", be as *neutral* as you can.
- **Feelings** – when sharing what you're experiencing, be as *authentic* as you can.
- **Thinking** – when saying what's working/not working, be as *candid* as you can.
- **Needs** – when requesting what you need, be as *clear* as you can.

Tim looked thoughtful. "I can see what you're saying about bringing neutrality, authenticity, candour and clarity into a conversation, but how do I do that?" he asked.

"It helps to practise," I suggested. "Begin by imagining that you're talking with Alison and she's listening carefully. What would you say?"

It took Tim a while to find his voice but once he got going, the words started to flow.

By the time he'd finished articulating his truth (see Figure 12), he looked 10 years younger. At the start of our session, he'd appeared tired and crumpled. Now his eyes shone, his back was straight and he stood tall.

Figure 12 – Tim's truth

"It's been two years since you made me Design Director. Since then, I've been taking a lead on handling client projects. My workload has increased significantly, so I often stay in the office until past 7pm. Last week, when you were on leave, I had to finish off the visuals that you'd asked Ian to complete for the new client, which took me until 10pm two nights in a row."

(Observations expressed as neutrally as possible)

"As a result of all the extra work I've been doing, I'm feeling frustrated at having to stay late so often. I'm annoyed at the way work is eating into my evenings and stopping me from doing my marathon training. I'm sad that I'm spending so little time with my family while our son's so young."

(Feelings expressed as authentically as possible)

"It's great that the business is doing so well and that we've got so many potential new clients. I think we have a great team of designers who are keen to learn more. What I think isn't working, however, is that you're not being realistic when you estimate how long a project will take. The jobs often take longer than you budget for, which makes scheduling difficult and means I often have to stay late to meet the deadlines."

(Thinking expressed as candidly as possible)

"What I'd like is to be involved in the scheduling decisions for proposals to new clients. I suggest we have a conversation every Monday morning to discuss the project pipeline and our top priorities. If you think you'll need me to stay late into the evening, I'd like to be told at least 24 hours before so I can plan for this and let my family know."

(Requests expressed as clearly as possible)

"How does this sound to you?"

(Response invited)

"There's one final thing," I counselled. "You need to find out what Alison's response is. Ask something simple like, 'How does this sound to you?' When we invite response, it helps to soften the impact of our truth telling."

"I feel like an athlete who's warmed up before a big event," Tim said. "Now that I've rehearsed what I want to say and how I want to say it, I'm ready to face Alison and have that Big Conversation."

Setting himself free

The final push to have the Big Conversation came when Tim was diagnosed with stress and high blood pressure. His wife had been concerned for some months that he'd not been eating or sleeping properly and sent him to the doctor. When Tim realized that not saying or doing anything about his demanding work schedule was affecting his health, he decided to face the music and talk with Alison.

Tim chose the moment for his Big Conversation with care. He arrived at the office early one morning, knowing that he'd find Alison alone working away at her computer. Once he checked she was OK to talk, Tim used OFT'N to voice his observations, feelings, thoughts and needs about the constant pressure he felt under and the changes he wanted. He spoke his truth with clarity and conviction and then asked Alison what she thought.

While Alison didn't agree with all Tim's requests, she acknowledged how hard he'd worked and how much she valued his contribution. Tim was surprised by how good it felt to receive this recognition because he'd had the courage to speak out.

A month later, while life at the office remained the same, Tim realized that the big change had occurred within him. By calling out his frustration, he'd got in touch with the reality of the situation and could see that he now needed to take further action. When he noticed an ad for a graphic designer in a studio near his home, he instinctively knew that this was his opportunity to create a new life for himself. When his application was successful, he accepted the position so he could realize his dream of training as a sports massage therapist in the hours he would have spent commuting.

Tim decided to resign by meeting Alison face to face instead of sending an impersonal email. With newly found confidence from having had a Big Conversation already, Tim felt more at ease in breaking the news of his career decision. All Tim's fears over many years about ruining the relationship with Alison or burning his bridges were unfounded. Not only did she give him a glowing reference, Alison also took the team out for a farewell party and Tim noticed, with a wry smile, that she was the first to offer to buy a round of drinks.

Summary

Speaking our truth can be uncomfortable but is essential to a Big Conversation. Truth telling is a two-fold process. First, we tell our truth to ourselves and then we tell our truth to another person. When we stand in our truth, we set ourselves free to be who we really are. You can do this by taking these steps:

- **Address the undiscussables**. Be honest with yourself about the conversations you've been avoiding. Ask yourself what it would take to turn the topics you think are taboo into something you could discuss, even with some discomfort.

- **Do a reality check**. Remind yourself that your truth is not the Truth. Distinguish between the objective reality (your observations) and your opinions about the situation (your thoughts). Challenge yourself to see the bigger picture.

- **Listen to your feelings**. Tune into how you are really feeling. Pinpoint which of the six core emotions you are experiencing (happiness, sadness, anger, envy, shame or fear). Be as precise as you can about the truth of what you are experiencing.

- **Have a R.A.N.T**. Tell your truth to yourself about the other person. Write down and complete the following statements: "I resent you for …", "I appreciate you for …" and "I need you to …". Read aloud your statements to see which ones resonate and which no longer ring true. Distil your truth.

- **Express yourself often**. Tell your truth to the other person using the OFT'N principle. Share your observations, feelings, thinking and needs. Own what you are saying using "I" statements, such as "What I think isn't working is …".

- **Walk your talk**. Rehearse for the Big Conversation by practising speaking your truth. Consider the actual words you'll use and how you'll say them. Attend to the tone. Be as neutral, authentic, candid and clear as you can.

- **Invite a response**. Once you've spoken your truth, ask the other person what their truth is. Drop your expectations and be open to what they say. Accept the possibility that nothing changes except who you are, which can then change everything!

Meaningful conversations

In a conversation, we can communicate at different levels. Talking with a stranger while waiting for a bus to arrive is not the same as with talking with our best friend. Our everyday interactions are often quite pedestrian, whereas Big Conversations demand more of us. Understanding the different levels on which we can communicate helps us to build rapport, create trust and deepen our conversation.

A useful model attributed to the psychologist Eric Berne (author of *Games People Play*) distinguishes between four levels of communication. As we progress up the levels, we become more engaged and the conversation is more energizing:

- **Facts and information**, such as sharing what work you do and where you live
- **Beliefs and opinions**, such as how we voted in the last election and why
- **Feelings and emotions**, such as expressing our frustration, joy or sadness

Moving up the levels not only makes our conversations more meaningful, it involves taking more risk. Research reported in *The Psychologist* (April 2005) reveals that we express our inner thoughts and feelings only 2 percent of the time in everyday conversations. To make our conversations less transactional and more transformational, we need to open up and speak our truth.

CHAPTER 9

Shift 6 –
Surrender your story

*"You are what exists before all stories.
You are what remains when the story
is understood."*

Byron Katie

A Big Conversation sometimes calls on us to step out of our "story". Our story is a tale we tell about ourselves, about others and about our situation that stops us from being who we really are. Whether it makes us feel small or superior, a victim or a villain, our story is what separates us from our real selves and from each other. When we become aware of this inner dialogue we can avoid sabotaging the conversation we're having with another person and allow new possibilities to emerge.

When our minds are full of thoughts about what "should" and "shouldn't" be happening, we're immersed in our story. It might be a tale of "This shouldn't be happening to me",

"They should apologize" or "I'm a failure". If we become overly identified with our story, we're not our true selves and our conversation is stunted.

When we feel hurt, upset or disappointed by something the other person says, we are getting into our story. When we attack back, withdraw in a sulk or throw a guilt trip, we are coming from our story. Our story can run our lives and ruin our conversations. The tentacles of our story can stretch from childhood, through adolescence and into adulthood. We often don't see how our story has grabbed hold of us and strangled our sense of who we are.

To surrender our story, we first need to become aware of it. We need to realize that there are two conversations running at the same time: the one we're having with ourselves and the one we're having with the other person. Becoming conscious of the invisible, unexamined, constant conversation going on inside us makes a huge difference to how we talk with another person and what happens as a result.

Once we're less identified with our story, we can be with the other person in a new way. We can talk with them without putting them in the wrong and without diminishing ourselves. In the expanded space between us, new insights emerge and we spiral into new possibilities. Changing our conversation by changing our story is what this chapter is all about.

Time to talk

You're on a mission to make a real difference to other people's lives through your work. You're not willing to stand by and pretend that there's no suffering in the world. At times, you've sacrificed your own well-being to help others. When colleagues have treated you unfairly, you've backed down and moved on to the next task.

In your current role, you're finding yourself in

a familiar situation: your boss is undermining you and you feel powerless to stop it. With a heavy heart, you are considering raising a formal grievance, but you're reluctant to go through what you know will be a protracted, painful process. You've tried to talk but you're not sure you have the time, capacity or inclination to talk further. However, you can't see any other way to air the issues, clear your name and find a resolution.

Teresa has found her way through a situation just like this.

Teresa is a hard-working, committed and energetic woman in her early forties. She believes passionately in her work to help the most disadvantaged people in the world. Her gentle smile and softly spoken voice betray a sensitivity striking for someone so driven. Half French and half English, she is expressive, articulate and engaging. When she's amused, her face lights up like a young child's. When she's annoyed, she attacks like an angry adolescent. Talking with Teresa is a roller-coaster ride.

Before becoming Director of Fundraising for a global charity a year ago, Teresa spent a decade working as a fundraising manager for a campaigning organization. Her outstanding track record of assisting disadvantaged people is marred by only one issue: a persistent pattern of being bullied. The saying "People join organizations but they leave managers" puts a grim smile on Teresa's face, as she left her last job after being persecuted by a member of the board. With her self-confidence in tatters, she decided to wipe the slate clean by starting with a new charity, spearheading their ambitious fundraising campaign.

To begin with, all looked rosy. Jim, her new boss, was delighted at having such an experienced new member of the team. He took her into his confidence and sought her advice about conflicts he was having with other colleagues. He tasked her with changing the culture of the organization to become more professional and efficient. Teresa went all out to create new strategies, secure high-profile sponsors and raise funds through corporate donations. She achieved some excellent results, fast.

After a few months, Teresa started to receive emails from Jim saying that some of the changes she'd made were making others feel uncomfortable. When she asked for more details, Jim went silent. Teresa also noticed that Jim was excluding her from key meetings with potential sponsors and withholding important information. He then refused to let her recruit another team member to handle the growing corporate portfolio, making her fund-raising targets almost impossible to reach.

Teresa is finding working for Jim increasingly intolerable. She's learned that he's been approaching members of her team for information even while they're on holiday or sick leave, without consulting her. He's criticized her openly more than once in front of her colleagues.

"I feel I'm being completely undermined," Teresa says. "I can't believe it, but I think I'm being bullied *again*."

When she's tried to have a conversation with Jim to discuss the issues, he's either not available or suggests they meet at a later date that never comes. Teresa is so frustrated that she's become hypervigilant for signs of wrong-doing by Jim, whom she now sees as manipulative, controlling and evasive.

Teresa recently received an email from Jim with a draft copy of her end-of-year appraisal. When she saw he'd given her an overall rating of "below standard", instead of the "excellent" she was expecting, she felt very angry. She's refused to sign it, seeing his assessment as inaccurate and a slur on her name. She believes Jim is ramping up the pressure to force her out of the organization.

Teresa is considering raising a formal grievance about Jim, but she knows that it would be a lengthy and painful process. She believes in the power of dialogue as a way to clear the air and resolve the appraisal issue, but she feels too demoralized to hope that it could still work.

It was at this point that Teresa got in touch with me for some coaching.

"I think the time to talk has come," she said. "But how can I make change happen through dialogue?" What follows is the answer we found to that question, step by step.

Marshal your resources

We become "stuck" when we're unable to make the next appropriate move in life. Whether this is to send off a job application, complete a dissertation or have a significant conversation, we often need some help to get "unstuck". When we find a way to reclaim our power, we can move forward.

At our first coaching session, Teresa told me of her history of being bullied at work. Her tears of frustration and outbursts of anger made it hard for me to follow the thread of her narrative. She seemed to slip out of our conversation and be transported back to painful times she'd experienced throughout her life. After exploring some of these memories, I encouraged Teresa to come back to the present and speak of the current challenges she was facing.

"Jim's out to get me," Teresa said, almost spitting out the words. "Him rating me as 'below standard' in my appraisal is a real show-stopper. I feel very aggrieved."

Teresa said that she was so demoralized that she didn't know if a resolution with Jim was possible.

"Nothing I do will change this," Teresa said, with real despair in her voice. "I feel absolutely helpless."

I let Teresa cry her tears and vent her anger. I sensed that once she'd been able to express her distress, she'd drop into a more peaceful place and I would only need to acknowledge her tough situation. I'd learned over the years that simply allowing someone to have their emotions was sometimes the best help I could give.

As Teresa calmed down, I found out that she was a trained mediator and had been successful in helping colleagues through difficult conversations. When it came to her own conflict, however, she seemed unable to help herself. It seemed to me that Teresa's lack of self-confidence was a real barrier to her having a productive dialogue with Jim.

Teresa related how colleagues had been taken advantage of her throughout her career. She evoked in me both compassion for the hard times she'd been through and a strong sense that she was deeply immersed in a story of feeling victimized and of pointing the finger of accusation at other people. She was being treated unfairly *and* she was feeling helpless to do anything about it. In order to have a robust conversation with Jim, I felt she first needed to strengthen her self-belief.

I asked Teresa to complete the Resources exercise (see Part III, pages 255–6). This would help her to identify the sources of support she could draw on to feel more confident about talking with Jim. Using the template given, Teresa mapped out the different people, places and information that would energize her to have a conversation with Jim and create some change. Figure 13 on page 170 shows the resources Teresa came up with.

When we explored her map together, I asked Teresa how she could use some of these resources to move forward. She identified three main actions that she could take:

1. **Talk with trusted colleagues and clients** – collect positive evidence of her successes. This would help to strengthen her self-confidence as well as be a source of evidence of her competence to present to Jim.

2. **Do some research** – find out about bullying and grievance procedures. Although making a formal

Figure 13 – Teresa's resources

complaint was not Teresa's preferred option, checking out whether she had a legitimate case could be clarifying.

3. **Talk with her trade union rep** – see what support the rep would be able to give Teresa for her conversation with Jim. Knowing her rights would help Teresa to stand in her strength even in an informal conversation.

Seeing that there was more support available than she'd realized, Teresa began to do something about her situation. She spoke with her colleagues, consulted her trade union rep and created a file detailing her fundraising achievements. Instead of telling herself how hopeless the situation was, she created some momentum for the Big Conversation. She was starting to step out of her story and into her life.

Look for the light

In addition to the support that is available in our *outer* world, our *inner* world also funds us with a wealth of resources for a Big Conversation. By leveraging our psychological capacities, such as resilience, optimism and empathy, we can actively make a conversation happen rather than passively watch our life slip by.

To help Teresa articulate her personal strengths, we began, somewhat paradoxically, by looking at what she perceived to be her areas of "weakness". Given that her self-confidence was at such low ebb, I felt this rather oblique approach would be more helpful to Teresa than trying to identify her strengths head on.

Our so-called weaknesses can sometimes be strengths with the volume turned up too high or too low. For example, aggression "turned down" can be assertiveness and compliance "turned up" can be responsiveness. By setting the volume at the right level, we can use these characteristics in a conversation rather than seeing them as foibles or faults.

Teresa identified three main areas of weakness. She said that feedback over the years from colleagues, family and friends had identified certain characteristics as problematic in some way.

I wanted to challenge her own perception of her personality, so that she could bring the whole of herself into the conversation with Jim. For each of her so-called weaknesses, I asked Teresa to articulate how it could, at times, be an asset. We then explored what she could do to leverage these untapped strengths when she had a Big Conversation with Jim. Where we got to is shown in Figure 14 on page 172.

Figure 14 – Teresa's inner resources		
Area of weakness	**How this can sometimes be a strength**	**How to leverage this strength**
I'm oversensitive.	I fight for the underdog.	By standing up for myself, expressing myself with calmness and clarity.
I'm impatient.	I'm driven to get things done.	By choosing the right time to have the conversation with Jim, rather than rushing headlong into it.
I take on too much.	I achieve excellent results.	By pacing myself to focus on resolving this issue, rather than spread myself too thinly and risk neglecting it.

Having looked at her "weaknesses" in a different way, I decided that Teresa was now ready for the next question.

"So what do you think are your three key strengths?" I asked.

Having done the earlier work, Teresa's response came quickly and easily. She spoke with great fluency of her integrity, her resilience and her passion to make a difference. By the end of our session, her eyes were shining and there was colour in her cheeks. We talked about how she could draw on these attributes when she had the Big Conversation with Jim.

"I'm in a stronger position than I thought," Teresa reflected.

"So let's see how you can strengthen your position further," I replied.

Change what's changeable

When we're facing a difficult conversation, it helps to focus on what we *can* change rather than being consumed by what we can't. It is all too easy to think, "He never listens", "She wants it on her own terms no matter what" or "These things always happen to me". To the extent that we're fixated on what's wrong with the other person, with the situation or with ourselves, we're likely to stay stuck in our story.

To create a change by talking with someone, we have to switch our focus to being positive, proactive and purposeful. "What you focus on expands" is a powerful principle that applies as much to having a Big Conversation as to other areas of life. When we put our attention on what's changeable, it generates energy for talking in a transformational way.

During our early sessions, I had been somewhat taken aback by Teresa's anger at having to seek coaching in the first place. She had come to me because she needed help, but she seemed resentful at being driven to find support.

"Why does the onus have to be on me to make a change? Jim's the one who's behaving appallingly!"

I shared with Teresa that I understood that Jim's behaviour was making her life very difficult, but changing him was out of our reach.

"We're focusing on you, here," I said. "Not because we're condoning Jim's behaviour but because, ultimately, you can only take responsibility for yourself."

I understood how Teresa might feel angry about having to take action herself, given her history of being bullied. I was, however, concerned that her constant focus on what was wrong with Jim would derail any dialogue she tried to have with him. In our conversations, Teresa would often slip into accusing Jim of being cruel and vindictive, as well as railing against the injustices of her performance appraisal and work place in general.

To help Teresa shift focus, I asked her to draw two circles on a piece of paper, one inside the other. In the smaller circle I asked her to write down what she could change herself, without the help of anyone else. In the outer circle, she was to write down what she could change only indirectly, through influencing others, for example.

As Teresa wrote down the things she could influence but not directly impact, she became very focused. When it came to jotting down the things that she could change herself, she was even more thoughtful. Figure 15 shows what Teresa came up with.

Figure 15 — Teresa's circles of influence

Becoming aware of what is ours to change is a powerful shift to make. If we believe that we're constantly at the mercy of other people, external circumstances or fate, we stay passive and purposeless. Psychologists have found an "external locus of control" to be associated with lower levels of well-being, mental health and success.

When we believe that we *can* change our response to what happens to us, we become more active. If we have an "internal locus of control", we're more likely to reach out to others, seek information and assume that we'll be successful. Shifting our focus from the "rocks" we can't move to the things we can change helps to get us out of a rut and into a conversation.

"Now I've looked at my situation through different eyes," Teresa observed, "I'm starting to feel more confident. Seeing that I have some control over what I say, what I think and what I feel makes the conversation with Jim more of a possibility."

Detach from the drama

When we find it challenging to have a constructive conversation, it might be because our story interferes with our ability to talk. Our story is sometimes like a soundtrack that keeps playing over and over in our head. Left unexamined, this inner soundtrack keeps steeping us in the drama of a situation. Instead of seeing what's possible, we become fixated on what's wrong. By bringing this internal dialogue into the light of awareness, we become more available for a robust conversation with another person.

Our story can be problematic in two main ways. Firstly, this inner soundtrack can leak into our conversation and sabotage it, without us even realizing. If our inner dialogue is full of hostility, for example, the other person is likely to pick up on this, even if we don't say anything that is explicitly antagonistic. Or, if our story is one of superiority, another person may cut short the conversation, turned off by the way they are made to feel small in our puffed-up presence.

The second way in which our story can disturb a conversation is that we can get so distracted by the voice inside our own head that we're not fully present to the other person. We may miss what they are communicating and find it hard to "think on our feet". Afterwards, we may chastise ourselves by thinking, "If only I'd said ...". At the time, however, we were more absorbed by what we were saying to ourselves than by what the other person was saying to us.

A Big Conversation can only happen when we are awake, alert and attentive to what is happening right *now*. It is only when we step aside from our story and into the present moment that transformational change occurs.

It can be a challenge to uncover our story, given that it lies buried in our psyche. To help Teresa become more conscious of her own inner workings, I suggested that she complete the Rewind exercise. This involved her writing out a conversation with Jim that she'd found painful and unproductive. Alongside the actual words that each of them said, Teresa also wrote down the thoughts and feelings that she *hadn't* expressed. Teresa's completed Rewind exercise appears in Part III, see pages 258–61.

At our next coaching session, Teresa and I read aloud the actual conversation she'd had with Jim, as well as her inner dialogue. As we went on to discuss their interaction (which I cover below), I noticed a big change in Teresa. Her shoulders relaxed and her face softened. Although she'd found it difficult, writing out the conversation had made her detach from the drama of the situation. Instead of being reactive, she was now being reflective.

This time, when Teresa recounted her history of being bullied by her bosses, I noticed that I could follow the thread of what she was saying more easily. Whereas before she'd swung between being accusatory and feeling victimized, she was now calmer and more coherent. I could imagine her talking with Jim in this more centred way. I sensed that if she could find a way of being in a similar state with him, their dialogue would be decidedly different.

It was with this in mind that I invited Teresa to go to the next level and step aside from her story.

See your story

In order to surrender our story, we first need to see it. The challenge is that often we are unaware that we have a story at all. As Byron Katie is fond of saying, "You have a story but you are not your story." Although our story is not who we really are, we need to see it and own it before we can move beyond it. For this reason, coming to terms with our story can be both uncomfortable and illuminating.

Our story usually has its roots in our childhood. Given how vulnerable we are when we are very young, many of us will have been traumatized without realizing it. For example, a dramatic parental loss of temper could be so distressing to a child that she becomes anxious whenever she hears raised voices. As she grows up, she finds it hard to stand up for herself and confront others. Her story becomes, "I mustn't rock the boat." What happened when she was three years old shapes what she thinks, feels and says (or doesn't say) to this day.

Not all stories are rooted in painful or disturbing childhood experiences. We may have internalized a message from our parents or teachers that inflates our sense of who we are. When it comes to having a Big Conversation, however, this story of "I'm always right" can be just as problematic as a story of "I'm a victim".

If we bring our story into our awareness, we can choose to

stop playing small or to stop acting superior. As a result, our conversations may never be the same again.

Our story is most easily revealed through our feelings. Returning to her Rewind exercise, I asked Teresa to underline the three strongest feelings she'd experienced while talking to Jim. Teresa identified these as:

- "I'm really anxious."
- "I feel completely deflated."
- "I feel ashamed."

Knowing that I might be treading on tender ground, I asked Teresa the next question gently. "When have you experienced these same feelings before?"

Teresa paused. "Many times," she said quietly, with tears in her eyes.

"What's the first time you can remember feeling anxious and ashamed?" I enquired.

After a long pause Teresa replied, "When I was six years old." Her voice was quiet and she looked down at the floor.

"I'd been out playing with a friend and had got home late. My father went into such a rage that I thought I'd never be allowed to go out again. When I started crying, he told me to shut up and sent me to my room. I stayed there 'til the next morning when my mum found me still crying."

Teresa went on to describe how she'd been verbally abused by her father throughout her childhood and into her teens. She said that she'd never really learned to stand up to him, even though she was now over 40 years old.

Choosing my moment carefully, I asked, as gently as I could, "What might the connection be between your father and Jim?"

Teresa looked me straight in the eyes. "I feel the same way around Jim as I felt with my dad," she said. "I have this overriding sense that, when things go wrong, it's all my fault."

"And how does that affect your conversations with Jim?" I asked.

"I swallow what I want to say instead of speaking it out loud," Teresa replied. "I come away from conversations with Jim feeling completely powerless."

Her eyes grew wider as she went on to say, "I've been feeling like I've been abused by Jim, but I'm starting to see that I've been *letting* him talk to me like that. If I changed the way I spoke to him, perhaps it would change the way he spoke to me."

Teresa was starting to disengage from her story of "It's all my fault." She was standing on the edge of a huge step in her ability to have a Big Conversation.

Stop the sabotage

Our inner dialogue, left unexamined, can undermine our ability to talk with another person. Our unexpressed thoughts and feelings write the real script for the conversation. If our thoughts are full of judgment, for example, this negativity will leak into our conversation, no matter what we say. If our thought pattern is supportive or more spacious, we are more able to listen and new possibilities can emerge as we talk.

To illustrate the power of thought patterns in conversation, David Bohm, the quantum physicist and author of *On Dialogue*, uses the metaphor of a polluted river. If we focus our efforts on cleaning the water, we will find that the river quickly gets contaminated again. It is better to "go upstream" and remove the toxins at source. Similarly, it is better to stop subverting a conversation by clearing up our thinking, rather than focusing only on how we talk.

A key capacity to cultivate is what David Bohm calls "suspending". This involves laying out our thinking in front of us so we can examine it, explore it and evaluate it. We can then see whether our thought patterns sabotage or serve the conversation. Suspending is a subtle skill and yet one of the most powerful to develop for a Big Conversation.

I shared with Teresa that, in my experience, there are three thought patterns that deaden a dialogue. To see if she was caught up in any of these, I encouraged her to review the unexpressed thoughts she'd written down as part of the Rewind exercise. Teresa found that there was evidence that her thinking was getting tangled up in all three:

- **Getting defensive** – "Why can't he appreciate that I'm already doing three people's jobs?"
- **Blaming yourself** – "I'm no good at speaking up for myself. He never listens to me anyway."
- **Accusing others** – "He always belittles me and rubbishes what I say."

"I had no idea all those thought patterns were running through my mind at the time," said Teresa. "No wonder I found it so hard to think on my feet."

I explained to Teresa that if such thoughts remain unexamined, they make it difficult to manage our conversation with another person. They create such a "cognitive load" that our inner talk competes with our external conversation and real dialogue becomes impossible. When we're more aware of our inner dialogue, we become more receptive to what's emerging in the conversation, which can have unexpected outcomes.

"It feels like the clouds are clearing in my mind," reflected Teresa. "But if those unspoken thoughts were sabotaging the conversation, what will help support it?"

It was that question that we addressed next.

Speak the unspoken

Becoming more mindful of our inner dialogue has other benefits. As well as dissolving unhelpful thought patterns, we may be able to integrate our intuition into our thought process. Our ability to understand something immediately, without the need for conscious reasoning, is an unparalleled ally when we're facing a Big Conversation. The challenge lies in accessing this sixth sense. Our intuition only arrives in the moment we need it.

In his work on dialogue, David Bohm underlined the importance of "proprioceptive awareness". This refers to being aware of, for example, a bodily sensation, as it's happening. By contrast, "retrospective awareness" is when we look back and realize that we felt our heart sink at a certain point in the conversation.

With proprioceptive awareness, we're able to notice a feeling or thought as it's bubbling up within us. We can then use this data to express what's arising in us at the time it will have most impact: the present moment. This makes us less likely to walk away from a conversation thinking "If only I'd said …", or "I wish I'd told them to …" or "If I'd had my wits about me, I'd have …".

Developing our proprioceptive awareness makes us better able to bring our intuition online when we're talking. Thinking about how our intuition showed up in previous conversation (even if we didn't act on it) is a good starting point.

With this in mind, I asked Teresa to review her Rewind exercise once more. This time I asked her to see what "nuggets" were in her inner dialogue, amid all the "noise". Nuggets are any parts of her inner talk that would have been helpful to bring into the external conversation with Jim. Teresa found three unexpressed thoughts that she decided were nuggets:

- **"I'm feeling nervous about bringing up my proposal."** Teresa reflected that voicing this, for example by saying, "I'm finding this a bit awkward but I'd like us to talk about …", would probably have helped to settle her nerves. As it was, she pushed her anxiety to one side, only to find that it increased as her conversation with Jim progressed.

- **"I need to set the scene here."** Teresa realized that she'd plunged straight into talking about her proposal rather than giving Jim the bigger picture. She could have said, "Let me give you some context here …", and asked, "What would you like from this conversation?" As she hadn't done this, Teresa felt like she was "on the back foot" throughout the rest of their interaction.

- **"I need to hold my ground."** In her own mind, Teresa was clear that the conversations about her disputed performance appraisal and about the future fund-raising were very different. She could have said, "These are two distinct conversations. Let's talk about them separately." In her opinion, not articulating this at the time contributed to the derailing of the conversation.

Exploring how she could have brought these insights into her conversation with Jim was a real eye-opener for Teresa. She saw how voicing her intuitions would enable her to make some powerful interventions in the conversation.

"The conversation would have been different because *I* would have been showing up differently," Teresa reflected.

Teresa told me how valuable she'd found the Rewind exercise to be. It had raised her awareness of how she could change the conversation, not by putting on any kind of mask, but by becoming more herself.

"That makes me feel good," Teresa said, smiling.

Hearing Teresa say this, I knew that she was now ready to have her Big Conversation with Jim.

Taking a stand

Teresa prepared for her talk with Jim as thoroughly as she could. She still felt very apprehensive about their conversation and wondered whether she'd be able to remember everything she'd learned in her coaching. She made some notes to take into the meeting, with prompts for what to say if she felt bewildered and froze.

After careful consideration, Teresa decided to invite the HR manager to join them. She felt that it would be helpful to have someone witness the exchange to help clear her name, as well as being a sign of her growing confidence. To her great relief, the HR manager said that she was happy to attend.

At the start of the conversation, Teresa stated the purpose of the meeting and what she hoped it would achieve.

"I'd like us to agree a way forward for my unsigned performance appraisal," Teresa said. "What would you like to get from this meeting?"

Teresa listened closely as Jim and the HR manager stated what they wanted from the discussion. Starting the conversation with each person "checking in" brought some structure to the dialogue and gave everyone a chance to get settled.

Unlike in their previous meetings, Teresa found that she was able to be with Jim without being distracted by her inner dialogue. She listened to what he had to say without defending herself or cutting him off. When he reviewed her progress against the fund-raising targets they'd agreed at the start of the year, she could see that she'd fallen short in a couple of areas.

When it was her turn, Teresa talked calmly and clearly. She explained to Jim that because she hadn't been allowed to recruit the extra resources she needed, she'd struggled to raise the funds in all the areas they'd agreed. Referring to the file of evidence she'd complied, Teresa showed how she'd excelled at bringing on board new sponsors with large donations in the pipeline.

To her surprise, Teresa noticed that she was starting to relax. She thought back to the work she'd done to identify her natural strengths and how even her "weaknesses" could serve her.

"I'm becoming a spokesperson for myself," she found herself thinking. She smiled inwardly as she noticed how her inner dialogue had shifted.

In the light of the evidence she presented, Jim agreed to review his rating of her performance.

"I can see how hard you've been working," Jim said, "including in areas that I hadn't known about."

He agreed to look again at her proposal to recruit additional team members over the next few years.

"Thank you," said Teresa. "It would be good to have a follow-on conversation once you've looked in detail at the proposal."

"There's one more thing," Jim then added, unexpectedly. "I wondered if you'd be willing to stand in for me at the global conference next month? I can't make it and I think you'd do a great job of speaking passionately about how we can assist disadvantaged people on behalf of this organization."

"I'd be delighted," Teresa replied, as she gathered up her papers and drew the conversation to a close, thanking Jim and the HR manager for their time.

As she walked out of the door, Teresa felt an unanticipated sense of pride. She was pleased with how she'd handled the meeting and relieved that all her hard work to prepare had paid off. She decided to call a friend to celebrate.

By coming to understand her story of "It's all my fault", Teresa had been able to let it go. Instead of blaming others, she could stand in her power. Through having a Big Conversation, she was able to clear her name, resolve an issue and, most importantly, be her true self.

Summary

To surrender our story, we first need to become aware of it. If we are more conscious of our inner dialogue, negative thought patterns and troublesome emotions, they are less likely to leak out. We will also be better able to access our intuition. The following steps will help you to surrender your story:

- **Marshal your resources**. Make the most of any external sources of support that will help you to prepare for the conversation. This could be talking with people you trust, gathering helpful information or making notes for yourself.

- **Look for the light**. Leverage inner resources, such as your optimism, sensitivity and resilience. Be clear what your natural strengths are. Look for the hidden strengths in your "weaknesses" and see what you can do to bring these out.

- **Change what's changeable**. Pay attention to what you can change in your situation rather than what you can't. Focus your energy on what you think, what you feel and what you say.

- **Detach from the drama**. Write down a previous unsatisfactory conversation you've had, including your unexpressed thoughts and feelings. Become more aware of your inner dialogue so that you become more reflective and less reactive.

- **See your story**. Identify the troublesome emotions you experienced during an unsatisfactory conversation. Ask yourself when you have felt these emotions before. See the connection and find out what makes you feel small or superior.

- **Stop the sabotage**. Identify where in your inner dialogue you were blaming yourself, accusing the other person or getting defensive. See if there is any evidence that the other person picked up on these thoughts, even if you didn't voice them.

- **Speak the unspoken**. Notice the helpful, intuitive thoughts that bubble up inside you during a conversation. Find ways of saying these out loud. Keep some of your attention on your positive inner dialogue when you talk with the other person.

Embracing our shadow

Our "shadow" refers to the parts of our personality that we have repressed or hidden in some way. Our anger, lust, jealousy and need to dominate, for example, often remain out of our conscious awareness until, perhaps, we get drunk or overtired. Our shadow side can then emerge and disrupt a conversation.

We are often brought up to express only those behaviours that are socially acceptable. The rest of our personality remains unacknowledged or we unconsciously project it outward onto other people. We see *them* as controlling, evil or aggressive, rather than look inside and find our own inner tyrant.

As Michael Daniels points out in his 2005 book *Shadow, Self, Spirit*, our shadow can also contain more positive qualities. As a result of our upbringing, we may find it difficult to be gentle, compassionate or spontaneous. When we are more aware of our shadow, we can integrate all the different aspects of ourselves. We can let go of our story, become who we really are and have more vibrant conversations.

CHAPTER 10

Shift 7 – Find closure

"Life is a never-ending beginning."

Gabrielle Bossis

Facing our unfinished business can bring about a Big Conversation. Whether it's about finding a resolution, seeking a deeper understanding or saying that we're sorry, a conversation can bring closure to something that's been consuming our energy. By communicating with another person, we may be able to draw a line under an unresolved issue so that we're free to move on with our lives.

Our thoughts, feelings and behaviours tell us when we're carrying baggage from the past. We may find ourselves gripped by fear, bristling with resentment or weighed down with regret. Sleepless nights, avoiding someone or distracting ourselves with constant activity or by anesthetizing ourselves with TV, drink or another favourite drug are all signs we're avoiding that Big Conversation. Whatever it is, our unfinished business disturbs our peace of mind.

The first step in finding closure is often confronting ourselves and admitting how unsettled we're feeling. We need to accept that the consequences of the conversation, both for ourselves and for others, are unknown. Deciding to follow our inner prompting to talk is essential, in spite of it being inconvenient, uncomfortable or unwelcome.

When unsaid things are hanging around, the second step is to reach out to someone. We have to find a way to talk person to person, rather than be driven by our own need to clear our conscience, get things off our chest and sort things out once and for all!

Despite these challenges, completing unfinished business can bring huge benefits to everyone involved. A relationship can be renewed as deep-seated hurts are healed. Releasing ourselves from feeling guilty, sad or angry frees up enormous amounts of energy. Talking together can be the start of a new beginning, as we make room for something else to come in. Finding closure through a Big Conversation is what this chapter is all about.

From crisis to conversation

You've put yourself out to help a loved one who's run into trouble. However, what you thought might be a short-term solution has turned into a stressful long-term situation. You're still willing to help but increasingly feel that you're being too accommodating. As the months pass, you become more and more resentful at the way your goodwill is being taken for granted and your own life is on hold. You know that you need to say something to clear the air, but you find it hard to handle such a sensitive situation. You feel that the absence of a constructive conversation is starting to damage your relationship with a person you still care about.

Carlos had to grapple with this very challenge.

Born in the UK to Chilean parents, Carlos is an articulate, fiery, charismatic man. He has bright, shining eyes and a warm, broad smile. At 38 years old, Carlos enjoys being a self-employed photographer, as this gives him a creative outlet for his aesthetic skills. He also has a flair for words and uses colourful language, which he knows can be cutting at times.

For most of his adulthood, Carlos has lived in Sheffield in the small terraced house in which he was brought up. Just before his father died, when Carlos was 20 years old, he asked Carlos to take on the mantle of responsibility for his mother and younger brother, then aged 10. Carlos took this responsibility very seriously and lived with his mother to make sure she was well looked after. On the rare occasions when he's been able to afford it, Carlos has escaped for a few weeks at a time by going travelling, as there is nothing he enjoys more than taking pictures of landscapes in foreign lands.

A year ago, when his brother's marriage broke up, Carlos agreed that he could move back in to sort himself out. Their mother decided to rent a nearby flat to make room for Antonio's two small children who come to stay at weekends. When their mother transferred ownership of the property to the two brothers, they decided to remortgage the house so that Antonio could pay off some of his debts. Antonio had fallen on hard times after the property market crash and the collapse of his building business.

Although Carlos adores his niece and nephew, he is finding this domestic arrangement a source of increasing tension. He often works at home and is fed up with having to tidy away his laptop and expensive photography equipment every weekend. He's irritated that he can no longer invite his girlfriend around at the weekend for a relaxed evening watching a DVD. However, his main bone of contention is that Antonio is always late with his monthly payment toward the mortgage and that the free childcare that Carlos provides, particularly his babysitting on a Saturday night, is taken for granted by Antonio as well as his ex-sister-in-law, Helen.

The final straw came several months ago when Helen dropped off the two children unexpectedly. Helen's childminder was ill and, on the spur of the moment, she decided to leave the children with their father so she could go to work. When they arrived unannounced, Antonio was not at home. Carlos was busy working on a big project with a tight deadline for an important client. He felt very annoyed that he was expected to drop his commitments in order to look after the two children.

Carlos later sent Helen a short, sharp text. He had often found her inconsiderate but, for the sake of his brother, had held his tongue. This time she had overstepped the mark and he had to say something. He'd missed his deadline and risked losing the client.

Given the pressures of his brother's divorce and financial problems, Carlos decided not to confront him about this incident. Given how angry he was feeling, Carlos didn't trust himself to have a constructive conversation with his brother. "It would have been more of a vomit than a dialogue," as Carlos put it.

As the months have gone by, his resentment about being crowded out by his brother has been brewing. Because of the promise he made to his dying father and the joint mortgage, Carlos knows he can't just ask Antonio to move out.

In the absence of a conversation, Carlos is feeling increasingly trapped and resentful. Real tension is building between him and Antonio. Carlos is concerned that one day he might explode with rage and cause irrevocable damage to his relationship with his brother, and also with his mother, nephew and niece.

"It feels like a big crash waiting to happen," is how Carlos described it when he got in touch with me for some coaching.

He went on to ask, "How can I have a conversation with my brother to resolve this conflict? How can I say what's been festering for months while keeping the family together?"

What follows is the answer we found to that question, step by step.

Follow your inner prompting

When important things have been left unsaid, we can feel guilty, regretful or fearful. These feelings, although unpleasant, can goad us into reflecting on the need to talk. For this reason, acknowledging *to ourselves* how we're feeling is an essential first step toward a Big Conversation with another person.

We ignore such feelings at our peril. Although we might try to push them away, they keep gnawing at us. Admitting how we're feeling, however uncomfortable this is, can spur us on to talk. And without the conversation, we may never be able to make our peace with the other person, or with ourselves.

At our first coaching session, Carlos spoke of how unsettled he was feeling about his relationship with his brother. They'd always been close, even though they had their ups and downs, but Carlos felt that over the last few months Antonio had been withdrawing from him. Recently, Carlos had invited Antonio to go to the pub to watch a European cup final and Antonio had made an excuse and spent the evening with his friend.

As Carlos spoke, it became clear how agitated he was feeling. Carlos himself seemed surprised at how much "heat" he had about his situation.

"I can't sit on these feelings any longer," he concluded.

I was curious why Carlos was feeling so upset and I asked him if he'd experienced a "non-conversation" before. By this I meant a time when he'd felt an urge to talk but hadn't followed it through. In my experience, non-conversations can be a real source of sadness, anger and guilt. We often don't pay much attention to them as, by definition, they're something that didn't happen.

"The day before my father died," Carlos shared with me, "we talked, but I was feeling so choked that I cut the conversation short. I wanted to tell him that I loved him, but I never said it. I've regretted not having that conversation ever since."

Carlos's concern about having a Big Conversation with his brother was now starting to make more sense. I could feel his sadness at losing the opportunity to say a proper goodbye to his Dad all those years ago.

"So what did you learn from the experience with your father?" I asked, as Carlos blinked away some tears.

"I guess I learned how much I can regret turning away instead of talking," Carlos said, slowly and thoughtfully. "I don't want to make the same mistake with my brother. Perhaps that's why this voice inside my head keeps saying, 'Talk to him'".

Carlos then asked, "But how can I trust this urge that I'm feeling? How do I know this is the right thing to do?"

"When there's a prompting inside that doesn't go away," I replied, "it's a good idea to listen."

"I feel that the trust between us has deteriorated over the past few months," Carlos reflected. "I've not been honest with him about how frustrated I've been feeling. He's been avoiding me because he knows I can sometimes lose my temper when we talk."

With that said, we turned our attention to exploring how Carlos could manage his outbursts of anger during his Big Conversation with Antonio.

Own your stuff

There are, in my opinion, several behaviours that undermine a Big Conversation. Exploding with rage, telling a lie and passing on gossip are all destructive to talking together. If our conversation is to be a success, we need to recognize how we might destroy it. Taking measures to mitigate these behaviours can pay huge dividends when the time to talk comes.

Whether our tendency is to go into a rant, give the cold shoulder or make sly remarks, we all have our "stuff" to deal with. Being honest with ourselves about our unhelpful behaviours may make us squirm but, as the saying goes, "If we always do what we've always done, we'll always get what we've always got."

For Carlos, the main challenge in a Big Conversation was to keep his anger in check. Describing himself as a "smouldering volcano ready to go off", Carlos was aware that his angry outbursts would sever any conversation he tried to have with his brother. Over the years they'd grown up together, Carlos had often lost his temper and Antonio had learned to walk away.

Since they'd started living under the same roof again, Carlos had tried to contain his frustration. While this appeared on the surface to keep the peace, Carlos described their current situation as "One big festering pool of unfinished business".

"But because he's my brother and my blood," Carlos said, "I can't just walk out. I need to have this conversation to clear the air, but without blowing my top."

To help Carlos shift from being angry and aggressive to calm and collected, I encouraged him to write down all the self-righteous things he might say to Antonio. When we reviewed these statements, it was striking that they all began with "You …".

I challenged Carlos to rewrite these statements, starting with "I …". When we own what we say rather than point the finger at the other person, a conversation becomes much more constructive. Figure 16 shows how Carlos responded to this challenge.

I shared with Carlos that I'd witnessed huge fires put out in conversation through the use of "I" statements. It seemed to me that the more Carlos could take responsibility for what he

Figure 16 – Shifting to "I" statements	
"You ... "	**"I ... "**
"You're always taking me for granted when I look after the kids."	"I feel resentful that you don't say thank you when I've taken care of the kids."
"You're making my life really difficult by taking over the house at the weekend."	"I feel crowded out and I'd like you to give me more space at the weekend."
"You've let me and the family down with your messy break-up."	"I'm sad about your marriage breaking up and about how difficult it is for the whole family."
"You're always late with the mortgage payments!"	"I have a lot of concerns that we might lose the family home if we don't keep up to date with the mortgage payments."

said, the less likely Antonio was to go into a stony silence and ignore him.

After a short pause, Carlos asked, "But won't it make the conversation too much about me?"

"We haven't finished yet," was my reply and with that we went on to explore the next piece of the puzzle together.

Enlarge your awareness

When our differences have created divisions, resolving issues can be tricky. There is often a temptation to focus on who said what or who did what to cause offence. But how we have erred in the past fades into insignificance compared with what we can create together in the future.

Paying attention to a positive outcome creates a forward thrust for a conversation. We are more likely to find common ground in what we want for the future than how we perceive the past. This is not about ignoring what's happened, but about keeping the emphasis on what *can* be done rather than what should have happened.

Returning to Carlos's concern about the conversation becoming too self-absorbed, I shared with him a useful way to keep a dialogue both future-focused and orientated toward the other person. In preparing for a Big Conversation, it's helpful to think through what we want on three different levels. I asked Carlos to think through what he wanted from the Big Conversation for him as an individual ("me"), for him and his brother ("us") and for the rest of his family ("them"). There is often a tendency to focus only on "me" without thinking through the consequences for others. Extending our awareness to include "us" and "them" means that our conversation is more likely to benefit all the different people involved.

Before our next coaching session, Carlos thought through the positive outcomes he'd like from his Big Conversation with Antonio. I reminded him that focusing on positive outcomes does not guarantee them, but does make them more likely to emerge. Carlos said that what he wanted was:

- **For me** – to live in a comfortable, relaxed home where I can do my work uninterrupted, invite my girlfriend round and share quality time with the family
- **For us (Antonio and me)** – for each of us to have our own space, manage finances responsibly and socialize together when we choose to
- **For them (the kids, Mum and Helen)** – Mum to enjoy weekends with the kids, Helen to know that she's got the weekends to herself and the kids to be well taken care of in a pleasant environment

"It's been helpful to think through what I want for all of us, not just for me," Carlos reflected. "This Big Conversation is not just about me venting or getting appreciation for everything I do for the kids."

Carlos went on to explain that using the frame of Me-Us-Them had also made him realize that there was a decision to be taken, not just feelings to express.

"I can see now that the silence between Antonio and me has led to procrastination. By avoiding talking, we've been sleepwalking into a crisis. Neither of us wants to make the big decision about whether to sell the house. We're both trapped by our indecision as much as by the situation."

As Carlos paused, I could see him gathering his thoughts.

"I'm also thinking that asking Antonio what he wants in terms of me, us and them would be a good place to start the conversation," he mused.

And with that I was in complete agreement.

Make it personal

While focusing on outcomes helps bring direction to a conversation, it is important to balance this with attention to the relationship. In our drive to get down to business, there is a risk that we might overlook the relational for the transactional.

Martin Buber uses some very clear language to make this distinction. He writes of two fundamental orientations to dialogue, these being:

- **An "I-It" attitude** in which we see the other person as a role or a resource for us to use in achieving our own ends, instead of talking to them as a human being.
- **An "I-Thou" attitude** in which we see the other person as a fellow human being, with feelings, dreams and ideas of their own. We talk to them as a person who matters.

A Big Conversation often requires a balance between an "I-Thou" and an "I-It" orientation. We have to talk to the other person with the same respect with which we would want them to talk to us, while covering the difficult topics that need to be discussed. The challenge is to find a way to sort things out while keeping the relationship intact.

In Carlos's case, I felt it would be helpful for him to combine consciously the two approaches as he prepared to talk with Antonio. I asked him to complete the Table exercise (see Part III, page 262–3) to help him to think through what the conversation needed to cover. I was concerned that, without doing this preparation, Carlos might steamroll Antonio in his drive to clear the air and resolve the domestic issues.

Using the metaphor of a table, I explained to Carlos that the I-Thou element was like the table legs that needed to be put firmly in place first. Then, once the foundation was solid, the top of the table, representing the I-It or transactional element, could be brought in.

Carlos and I talked through how he could first attend to his relationship with Antonio. To talk with him *as* his brother, not just as the person with whom he shared the mortgage and childcare, I suggested that Carlos communicate two things:

- **Say why the conversation matters** – by speaking from his heart about how much their relationship meant to him, Carlos would bring sincerity into the conversation from the start.

- **State his part** – by baring his soul and owning up to his own shortcomings and the way he'd contributed to the need for them to talk, Carlos would make Antonio more likely to connect with him than if he displayed only his strengths.

I then asked Carlos to be clear about what he and Antonio needed to discuss with regard to their domestic practicalities. I suggested that he try to cover no more than three different negotiations in the conversation. More than that could be overwhelming for them both.

Using the template given in the Table exercise, Carlos outlined the relational and transactional elements of his conversation with Antonio, as shown in Figure 17.

"I'd not really thought about starting by saying why it's important to talk," Carlos reflected. "I've tended to just dive in when stuff has come up. Now I can now see how a different approach could lead to a different result."

After a pause Carlos said, "This Big Conversation feels like it will be a real stretch for me. There's a lot for us to cover in order to draw the line under what's happened and start again. If I could

Figure 17 – The relational and transactional elements of Carlos's conversation

WHAT WE NEED TO TALK ABOUT ...

- Childcare arrangements at the weekend, including last-minute changes
- Making the monthly payments toward the mortgage on time
- The use of shared living space, especially at weekends

This conversation matters because ...	My part in this has been ...
... you're my brother. ... the kids need a home at the weekends. ... keeping the family home is important for all of us.	... not speaking out when things have annoyed me. ... being short-tempered and self-righteous at times. ... not appreciating how stressful it's been for you.

accept the uncomfortable situation we're in, I think it will make talking with Antonio a lot easier."

And with that, we had our next step.

See the perfection

Making peace with ourselves before a Big Conversation can make a real difference to how we talk together. By truly accepting the need to talk, we can turn a crisis into a means of finding closure.

I was keen to help Carlos "see the perfection" in his decision to talk with Antonio.

Because he'd been putting it off for months, there had been a real build-up of unfinished business. I sensed that if Carlos could place the Big Conversation in a wider context, it would make talking with Antonio more meaningful and less demanding.

To help Carlos take a different perspective, I suggested that we explore what the learning opportunity might be for him in the current situation. I explained that while he may not have consciously chosen the situation he found himself in, there are other levels of creativity at work. I pointed out that our conscious creativity is like the tip of an iceberg that we can see, whereas other realms of consciousness are out of sight but just as present (see Figure 18).

Carlos and I explored how these three levels of creativity might have given rise to the need for a Big Conversation with Antonio:

- At the **conscious** level, we take decisions in full awareness of what we're doing. For example, Carlos had made the conscious decision to keep quiet about how annoyed he was about the late mortgage payments. Although this decision had made sense at the time, it had led him to feel very frustrated, hence the need to talk.

Figure 18 – Three levels of creativity

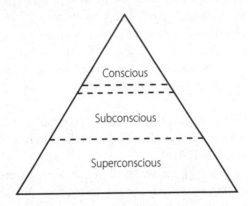

- At the **subconscious** level, we have thoughts that we're only dimly aware of but that are impactful nonetheless. Thoughts such as "I'm fed up that I've got hardly any space to myself in my own home" had contributed to the build-up of tension, even though Carlos had never voiced them or paid them much attention.

- At the **superconscious** level, we have an inner knowing that arises from a deeper place inside us. It is at this level that our soul speaks to us, through feelings, synchronicities and intuition, and also through the configuration of circumstances in our lives.

To help Carlos better understand the superconscious, we explored how the inner prompting he felt to talk with Antonio, and years before with his Dad, could have bubbled up from this level. Our superconscious knows the next step we're to take, including in our conversations, *whether we take it or not*. This is why we sometimes feel out of sorts when we don't talk with someone. On some level we know it's what needs to happen for our future to unfold, even though we resist it.

I explained to Carlos that I believe our superconscious holds the blueprint of our lives and reveals it to us piece by piece. Our superconscious brings us the perfect people, places and things that we require in order to evolve into the person we need to become.

"So, if you imagine that on some level you've created this whole scenario with Antonio and the kids," I asked, "what might you be looking to learn?"

There was a long pause. "Well, if this Big Conversation is about me learning to manage my anger, stop being so self-righteous and see everyone else's point of view, then I guess it's a perfect scenario," said Carlos, thoughtfully.

"And what difference does it make to view the Big Conversation in that way?" I enquired.

Carlos was quiet for a few moments. "The conversation would be a way of finding closure on what's been left unsaid *and* it could catapult me out of feeling so stagnated."

There was an even longer pause.

"Perhaps this conversation could even be a new beginning."

Invite co-creation

A true conversation is a co-creation. What gets spoken emerges out of our shared space. There are no fixed outcomes, pre-determined answers or guaranteed results in dialogue. When we let the conversation go where it will, talking together is full of potential.

I believe that this unpredictability is also what makes many of us withdraw from conversation. Giving up the illusion of being in control is not something that we find easy to do. However, when we find a way to loosen our grip on what needs to happen when we talk, we open ourselves up to new possibilities that we'd never reach on our own.

To help Carlos achieve closure with Antonio on the past and let his Big Conversation be the start of something new, we explored what it might mean for his own future. The more open-minded Carlos could be, the more likely it would be that the Big Conversation would be an aperture for new life to flow through.

Carlos reflected that the Big Conversation could be a turning point for him. Having spent the last 20 years living in the family home, life had been very comfortable. More recently, he'd been living off his share of the capital released when he and Antonio remortgaged the house, so his life had been even easier.

"But I think it's made me lazy," Carlos confessed. "And now I feel like I'm in a trap.

"I need to have my own space, but I can't see how I can earn enough to get a place of my own. I can't ask my brother to move out without feeling that I'm letting him and the kids down, as well as my mum and dad."

As I listened to Carlos, I became aware that he was making several assumptions. While it was true that he had supported his brother financially since the break-up of his marriage, Antonio was in fact legally entitled to half the house. Carlos seemed to be assuming that he had a moral right to a greater share of the family home given the support he'd been providing.

I shared this observation with Carlos and went on to say that it sounded like he was also making an either/or assumption. Either he needed to find his own place that would come at a cost that he wasn't sure he could afford, or he had to ask his brother to move out, which would feel like a betrayal given the promise he'd made to his Dad 20 years ago.

Carlos agreed that these were the assumptions he'd been making, without realizing it. I responded by saying that such assumptions usually lurk in the subconscious, where they go unnoticed. Once Carlos had brought his either/or thinking into full awareness, he was more likely to be able to release it. Assumptions can hamper a conversation because they limit the space of possibility in which we talk.

I suggested to Carlos that he invite Antonio to think with him about the future as they had their Big Conversation. They might come up with an idea that neither of them could have imagined on his own. New perspectives, solutions or insights turn talking together into a true conversation.

"So what you're saying is that there will be a creative solution to this situation?" Carlos checked. "And that it's through conversation that it's most likely to emerge?"

"Absolutely," I replied.

"That makes me feel alive!" Carlos smiled.

And with that, I knew he was ready for his Big Conversation.

Stepping onto new ground

A couple of weeks later, Carlos asked Antonio if they could talk. An inner prompting told him that it was a good moment one evening after work, when they were both relaxing at home. Without the kids or mum there, he knew it would be easier for them to have their Big Conversation, even if he still felt a bit nervous about getting it started.

"It really matters to me that we find a way to talk about us living together," Carlos began. "Finding a way for us to live well together is not only about you and me, it also affects the kids, Helen and Mum."

To Carlos's surprise, Antonio didn't clam up like he usually did. Taking this as a positive sign, Carlos continued.

"I know we've had our differences in the past. I've not always been able to keep my temper when things have annoyed me. I realize things have been very stressful for you lately and I can be a bit self-righteous at times."

Antonio nodded and said he was happy to talk. When it came to discussing the arrangements with the kids at the weekends and the late mortgage payments, Carlos was careful to use "I" statements rather than put Antonio in the wrong for what he'd done. Carlos kept calm, voiced his frustration and asked Antonio what he thought.

His brother apologized for the financial mess he was in and for the state of the house at the weekends. He said that he was grateful for Carlos's support at such a difficult time. Antonio then paused before making his next comment.

"I think this is the first time we've spoken about our differences without you blowing your top," he said.

Carlos thought back to his coaching sessions and wished he'd taken them 20 years ago.

As they carried on talking, Antonio confided that he was becoming increasingly concerned about the kids needing a proper home.

"I'm wondering whether there might still be life in my relationship with Helen," he confessed. "I'd like to give it another go, but don't know how to talk with her. Do you think you could help me think through how to have the conversation with her?"

Carlos nearly fell off his chair and said that he was more than happy to agree. They decided to discuss it over a drink the next time they went to the pub together.

The next day, Carlos looked back at the talk he'd had with Antonio the previous evening. He realized that while he'd thought it would be about negotiating childcare arrangements and financial transactions, it had actually been more about getting his relationship with his brother back on track.

Heartened by their talk, Carlos helped Antonio prepare for his conversation with Helen. Several months later, when the couple moved back in together, the brothers agreed to rent out the family home. Carlos decided to take up an assignment as a freelance photographer in Chile, a country he'd always wanted to visit. With his own life opening up before him, Carlos was overjoyed to realize that his Big Conversation had changed everything.

Summary

Completing our unfinished business is essential to living life well. It releases blocked energy, renews our relationship and ushers in a new beginning. Following these steps will help you to find closure through having a Big Conversation:

- **Follow your inner prompting**. Acknowledge the urge you're feeling to talk with someone. Listen to this feeling, particularly if it doesn't go away. Don't ignore this message; you may regret not talking.

- **Own your stuff**. Identify how your own behaviours or emotions might undermine a conversation. Take some ownership for what you say by using "I …" statements instead of "you …" statements.

- **Enlarge your awareness**. Look for common ground. Focus on the future more than the past. When you identify the positive outcomes you want from the conversation, think about what you want for yourself *and* for the other people involved.

- **Make it personal**. Attend to your relationship with the other person, not just the topics to be discussed. Share with them why the conversation matters to you. Show the same respect to them that you would like to receive yourself.

- **See the perfection**. Accept that the conversation is one piece of the larger mosaic of your life. See how the conversation could be the perfect next step in your own evolution.

The power of positivity

Positive emotions and behaviours help people and conversations to flourish. Feeling grateful, showing enthusiasm or saying what we like makes us happier, healthier and more resilient. Positivity is linked with living longer, having a more successful partnership and a stronger immune system.

Negativity in a conversation occurs when we get irritable, show contempt or express disdain. People who experience such troublesome emotions are more likely to describe their conversations as "hollow" and "empty". Negativity is also associated with taking more days off sick, worse physical health and poorer relationships.

Research published by Barbara Fredrickson and Marcial Losada in the *American Psychologist* (2005) shows that the balance of positivity to negativity is crucial. In a healthy conversation, there are three or more positive statements for every negative expression. This 3:1 ratio reflects that "bad is stronger than good". When the toxicity of a negative statement is outnumbered by appreciative comments, it can change our conversation and change our life.

- **Invite co-creation**. Let go of any assumptions you're making about the outcome of the conversation. Acknowledge that the best solution might emerge out of the space between you and the other person. Invite them to do some thinking with you.

Part III

The Know-How

A note about the exercises

These exercises have been designed to help you to prepare for a life-changing conversation.

To make the most of them:

- Do them on your own in a place where you won't be interrupted.
- Allow sufficient time – a minimum of 30 minutes per exercise, if possible.
- Make sure you have everything you need to hand before you start, such as a pen and plenty of paper.

You do not have to work your way through all the exercises if you don't want to. Sometimes just doing one is enough to create the shift inside that's needed. Enjoy this part of the book – and the changes it will bring!

EXERCISE 1

···

Backtrack

The purpose of this exercise is to help you to access the courage that you already have. It invites you to reflect on the times you have shown courage in the past, including in your conversations, to encourage self-belief and identify the strategies that work for you. It also invites you to identify times when you didn't show courage, so that you can learn from those experiences and make different choices in the future.

Timeline

1. Draw a horizontal line to represent your timeline from birth to the present day.

2. Mark on the timeline the ages at which turning points happened in your life (for example: age 18 left home; age 21 started first job; age 32 married; age 52 opened own business; age 60 went travelling). Aim for up to 10 turning points.

3. If the turning point called for some courage, draw a

vertical line above the timeline. The more courage you showed, the longer the line should be.

4. Focus on the three longest vertical lines. Taking each one in turn, ask yourself:

- What was the obstacle to be overcome?
- What strategy helped you to call up your courage?
- How did you feel as a result?

5. On your timeline identify the turning points when you felt you did not act courageously and draw a vertical line *below* the timeline. The more difficult you feel it was to call up your courage, the longer the line should be.

6. Focus on the three longest downward lines. Taking each one in turn, ask yourself:

- What was the obstacle to be overcome?
- What stopped you from calling up your courage?
- How did you feel as a result?

Reflection

After completing this exercise:

- What have you learned about what courage means to you?
- How do you feel you have grown by having or *not having* courageous conversations?
- What insights will you take with you to help you the next time you have to call up your courage for an important conversation?

....

Trade-off

*The purpose of this exercise is to help you come to a
clear and courageous decision about whether to have
a conversation or not. It invites you to think through
the risks and benefits of having the conversation, and
of staying silent. It also explores the other options that
are available.*

1. Think about the challenge and the conversation that you
   are contemplating having.

2. Define clearly the two options you are choosing between.
   Option A is to have the conversation and Option B is to
   stay silent. For Option A, identify who the conversation
   would be with.

3. Taking Options A and B in turn, write down their risks
   and benefits.

Option A

Have the conversation with . . . . . .

Risks   Benefits

. . . .

. . . .

. . . .

. . . .

. . . .

. . . .

Option B

Stay silent

Risks   Benefits

. . . .

. . . .

. . . .

. . . .

. . . .

4. Once you have explored both options, take some time out. When you are feeling refreshed, reflect on what you've written. Ask yourself if there any other options. Could you, for example, write a letter? Is there someone else you could have a conversation with first?

5. Imagine yourself in a year's time having had the conversation (Option A) and having stayed silent (Option B). In each scenario:

   - How would you feel?
   - What would you be thinking?
   - What would you and others be doing?

6. Make a clear choice about which option to take. Call up your courage and embrace your decision to have the conversation or to stay silent. Know that making a conscious decision will bring a sense of relief, and remind yourself that new decisions can be made as your life unfolds.

Inner-view

The purpose of this exercise is to inspire you to call up your courage in spite of any fears you may have. It invites you to have a conversation with the part of you that is courageous. If you take the time to tune in and listen, this exercise will connect you with your own innermost wisdom. Be amazed at what Courage has to say to you!

1. Relax, close your eyes and take some deep breaths. Place your attention inside yourself. Notice the rhythm of your heart beating. When you are centred, remember a time when you felt courageous (completing the Backtrack exercise, pages 211–12, will help you with this). Recall the physical sensations in your body and how you felt as you accessed your courage in that moment.

2. Get ready to have a conversation with the part of you called Courage. Notice if an image comes to mind, whether this be an animal, a person or something else. Let your imagination flow. Allow the experience to develop without trying to steer it. Start by saying,

"Hello, Courage. Can we talk?".

3. Wait for a response. If you don't hear one, make one up as best you can. This exercise is all about using your imagination in an active way. Write down the words you say and the words you receive in response.

4. Now, if it feels right, say, "What do you have to say to me? I will listen to you." Then listen to Courage's voice of wisdom.

5. Allow the conversation to unfold as an interactive dialogue between you and Courage. Write it down.

6. Don't try to control the conversation. Notice the feelings that come up. If you're not feeling anything, you're probably staying detached and watching from a distance rather than really participating. If you are not able to step into the conversation fully, put the exercise to one side and have a go another time.

A conversation with Courage

Here is Mary's conversation with Courage. At the time of writing she was feeling downhearted and uneasy about the prospect of having a conversation with her fiancé, Thomas.

Mary	Hello, Courage. Can we talk?
Courage	Of course. I am all here.
Mary	What do you have to say to me? I will listen to you.
Courage	I'm an old friend and a formidable foe. Friend to you and foe to the dishonest brokers in your life.

Mary	Who are the "dishonest brokers"?
Courage	Anyone who would do you down behind your back and try to take away your peace of mind.
Mary	And how are you a foe to them?
Courage	Because I keep you free to be you. I keep you moving forward.
Mary	And what else would you say to me, Courage?
Courage	To always have me close by, as one who lives in your heart and on your shoulder.
Mary	On my shoulder?
Courage	So I can see and scan the horizon for you and be ready to swing into action whenever the moment calls for it.
Mary	Why do you sometimes feel so far away?
Courage	Because you haven't befriended me. I'm a constant companion when I'm asked to be.
Mary	How can I befriend you more?
Courage	By calling on me and trusting me to do my work. I move in power when the time comes. I bring change, sometimes a complete turnaround, but never trauma, tragedy or terror.
Mary	What happens when I call on you, Courage?
Courage	I open the door of the cage for you. The real you can then emerge and take flight. With the wind beneath your wings, you will ride the air currents with joy.

. . . .

Homepages

The purpose of this exercise is to enable you to ground yourself before you have a conversation. It will help you to be clear about what you need to express. At the end, there are also some questions to help you build a bridge between your own container and the container you'll create with the other person.

Becoming still

1. Place your body in a comfortable posture. Keep your back straight and, if sitting on a chair, put your feet flat on the ground with your arms and legs uncrossed.

2. Focus your attention on your breath. Breathe in a quality you'd like to receive, such as peace. Breathe out any energy you want to release, such as anxiety. Do this several times until you feel your breathing slow down.

Journaling

3. Bring to mind the conversation you're contemplating and the person/s you would be talking with. See in your mind's eye the place where the conversation is likely to take place.

4. Write out and complete the following sentence, jotting down the first thing that comes to mind:

> "I am thinking about ..."

5. Write down another sentence and keep your hand moving across the page. Don't read back what you've written, just keep going. Carry on writing until you've filled a whole page. If the writing is still flowing, turn to a new page and keep on going.

6. Take any one of the following incomplete sentences and, as before, use it to start writing. Keep the writing flowing. Once you've filled the page, choose another sentence and complete it by writing whatever comes to mind, *without thinking about it*. You can use all the sentences or select the ones that stand out for you in some way:

> "I am feeling ..."

> "I am not feeling ..."

> "What I know is ..."

> "What I don't know is ..."

Reflection

Look back over what you've written. Bring to mind again the conversation you're contemplating. Reflect on the following questions:

- What is surfacing in my writing about this situation?
- What do I want to share with the other person/people about what I've written?
- What might stop me from sharing this? How can I overcome these obstacles?

EXERCISE 5

....

Discernment

The purpose of this exercise is to help you to prepare for a conversation. It invites you to think through what you want to express or speak for (advocacy), what you want to explore (enquiry) and what is best put to one side (bracket). Bracketing enables you to put aside consciously the things that are best left unsaid, so you can focus on what matters most.

1. Write in the table opposite the actual words you might use in the conversation. Use the subheadings in each of the three sections if they are helpful to you, otherwise feel free to discard, change or add to them.

2. Review what you've written in the table to see if it resonates. Make any amendments as needed. In the Enquiry column, make sure you've included, as far as you are able, open questions (i.e. questions that begin with "What ...?", "How ...?", "When ...?", "Why ...?" and "Who ...?").

BRACKET	
What's best left unsaid	
Accusations and judgments	

ADVOCACY	**ENQUIRY**
My feelings, thoughts, desires and requests	**Open questions that I genuinely don't know the answer to**
The hard truths	About me
The lost and forgottens	About the other/s
The never-before-saids	About our relationship

Cargo

The purpose of this exercise is to help you to decide in advance on your "cargo" – the energies or qualities you want to take into the conversation. It also invites you to identify the preoccupations that you want to leave behind. The state of being you take into a conversation charges the container with positive or negative energy.

Your three energies

1. Decide how you want to *be* for this conversation. Identify three energies or states of being that you want to carry into the conversation. Think of them as the energetic provisions that will be fuelling you. Write these on three separate pieces of paper. For example, you may decide to take with you:

Trust	Strength	Understanding

Here is a list of other states of being that you may consider as your cargo. Feel free to add others:

Acceptance	Grace	Patience
Authenticity	Gratitude	Peace
Cheerfulness	Honesty	Power
Compassion	Humour	Openness
Courage	Kindness	Spontaneity

2. When you go to the conversation, carry the three pieces of paper with you in your pocket, wallet or handbag. Keep them close by as a reminder that they are what you are consciously choosing to bring with you.

Your three preoccupations

Now decide which preoccupations you want to leave out of the conversation. Identify three things that could disrupt talking with the other person and are best left at home. Write these on three separate pieces of paper. For example, you may decide to leave behind:

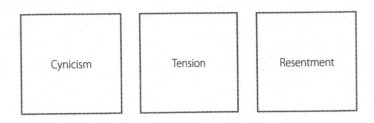

Here is a list of other preoccupations you could leave behind.
Feel free to add others:

Apathy	Judgment	Rigidity
Confusion	Panic	Sarcasm
Cowardice	Possessiveness	Shame
Guilt	Rage	Spite
Impatience	Regret	Uptightness

3. Decide where you will leave these three preoccupations.
   You could put them away in a drawer, bury them in the
   garden or give them to a friend for safekeeping. Choose
   what's best to do with them, whether it's to retrieve them
   at a later date, get rid of them for good or offer them up
   to the gods as a burnt offering. Notice how you feel when
   you release yourself from this unwanted cargo.

....

Threshold

The purpose of this exercise is to help you identify what it will take for you to cross the threshold into a new chapter of your life. It will enable you to have more clarity of intent about having a conversation.

1. Take a few moments to get as physically comfortable as you can. Sit cross-legged or in a chair with your back straight and your feet flat on the ground. Settle into being still. Close your eyes and notice yourself breathing.

2. Imagine you're writing the autobiography of your life. Bring to mind the contents page of the book, where the chapters are listed. What is the title of the chapter that relates to the present? Open your eyes, watch your hand pick up your pen and write down the title.

3. Take a fresh sheet of paper. Ask yourself, "What is the title of my next chapter?" Take a moment or two and let the title come to you, rather than thinking too hard. Watch as your hand takes the pen and writes down the chapter title on the new sheet of paper.

4. As you look at this chapter title, notice how it makes you feel. If it strikes a chord and you feel good, stay with it.

If it doesn't, is there a title that will make you feel a little bit better?

5. Put the two sheets of paper in front of you, with the current chapter on the left and the next chapter on the right. Take a third piece of paper and place it in the middle. At the top of this piece of paper write, "Threshold". Write down what you will have to do to end the current chapter and enter the next. What conversation, if any, is at this threshold? What will it take for you to have this conversation? Make some notes in response to these questions.

Current chapter	Threshold	Future chapter

Repertoire

The purpose of this exercise is to enable you to increase your conversational skills. It will help you to identify your strengths as well as the skills that you might need to hone.

Questionnaire

1. Bring to mind some recent conversations you've had with someone whom you want to talk with more effectively. Taking each of the sets of four statements in the questionnaire in turn, put a tick next to the statement that is *most* true of you:

A) Suggested what to talk about. ☐

B) Supported something the other person said. ☐

C) Clearly stated that you had a different point of view. ☐

D) Made an observation about the conversation itself. ☐

A) Proposed a topic for the discussion. ☐

B) Agreed with something that the other person said. ☐

C) Directly challenged what the other person said. ☐

D) Commented on how the conversation was unfolding. ☐

A) Initiated the conversation or part of it in some way. ☐

B) Said that you were in favour of something the other person said. ☐

C) Countered what the other person was saying with a contrasting point. ☐

D) Said something about the conversation as if you were a fly on the wall. ☐

A) Suggested that you move on to talk about something else. ☐

B) Made it really clear that you liked what someone else said. ☐

C) Provided an alternative opinion. ☐

D) Shared what you were noticing about how you were talking together. ☐

A) Provided a new subject to talk about. ☐

B) Encouraged the other person to say more. ☐

C) Stated another way of seeing an issue. ☐

D) Took a step back from an issue to look at the bigger picture. ☐

Move, follow, oppose or bystand?

2. Count up the number of As, Bs, Cs and Ds you have. Using the table on pages 232–3, identify which of the four actions of move, follow, oppose and bystand you are most likely to have used. This indicates your area of strength and the qualities that you bring to a conversation, as well as the unintended impact you may have if you overplay this strength. There are some suggestions as to what you can do about this (see pages 232–3).

3. Now go back to the questionnaire, read through each of the sets of four statements again and put a cross next to the statement that is *least* true of you. Count up the number of As, Bs, Cs and Ds. Using the table on page 233, identify which of the four actions is most likely to be missing from your conversation. Complete the relevant sentences with actual words you could use in your next conversation with the person you have in mind.

Mostly	The action you are most likely to make	The unintended impact if overplayed	How to hone your skill
A	A **move** to initiate a discussion, bringing: • Direction • Focus • Purpose	You may come across to others as being: • Pushy • Dictatorial • Impatient	• Once you've suggested a topic, check you have agreement to talk before proceeding. • Invite others to make a move by asking, "What would you like us to talk about?".
B	A **follow** by agreeing with the other person, bringing: • Completion • Harmony • Connection	You may come across to others as being: • Placating • Compliant • Wishy-washy	• Once you've established some common ground, make it clear where you see differences. • Be clear in advance on what you'd like to make a stand about and go for it.
C	An **oppose** by disagreeing, bringing: • Correction • Realignment • Challenge	You may come across to others as being: • Critical • Objectionable • Attacking	• State what you want to move toward, not just away from. • Give your reasons for disagreeing.

D	A **bystand** by observing *how* you are talking together, bringing: • Perspective • Neutrality • Context	You may come across to others as being: • Disinterested • Withdrawn • Aloof	• Signal that you are making a different kind of contribution by saying, "I want to shift gears here". • Be willing to put your voice in the mix and not just stay on the sidelines.

Mostly	What might be missing	How to activate
A	A move, to initiate a discussion	"I suggest we talk about . . ." "Let's discuss . . ." "How about we . . .?"
B	A follow, to agree with what the other person is saying	"I agree that . . ." "I support your suggestion to . . ." ". . . sounds great!"
C	An oppose, to disagree with the other person.	"I'd rather . . ." "I see . . . differently." "My challenge is . . ."
D	A bystand, to give a wider perspective.	"I'm noticing that . . ." "What I'm observing is . . ." "It looks like . . ."

EXERCISE 9

....

Elevation

*The purpose of this exercise is to help you to
have clear intentions for your conversation and
to release any expectations. You are invited to
elevate your intentions to "acceptances"
so that you can keep on interacting with
the other person even if your intentions
aren't realized.*

1. Bring to mind the conversation you want. Write any
   expectations you have about the conversation in the
   left-hand column of the table opposite (or copy
   this table onto a separate piece of paper). These
   expectations may be positive, such as thinking that the
   other person will agree with you, or negative, such as
   assuming that you'll clam up or that the conversation
   will damage your friendship. Think through your
   expectations about yourself, about the other person
   and about your relationship.

2. Taking each expectation in turn, elevate it into an
   intention. Instead of focusing on a specific outcome,
   write a broader statement of positive intent in the
   middle column of the table opposite. Write one

Expectations	Intentions	Acceptances
For me	For me	For me
For the other person	For the other person	For the other person
For our relationship	For our relationship	For our relationship

intention for yourself, one for the other person and one for your relationship. Make your intentions specific, positive and purposeful.

3. Return to your expectations for the conversation. Get some scissors and cut along the dotted line so that you remove the Expectations column. Throw this piece of paper away. Notice how you feel as you release your expectations.

4. Now take another look at your intentions. Ask yourself what you can accept, even if it's not your preference. Insert some statements in the right-hand column.

EXERCISE 10

Triggers

The purpose of this exercise is to help you to manage any troublesome emotions you experience when you talk with another person. Being more aware of what gets you "triggered" will help you to identify some coping strategies to make you more relaxed and less reactive.

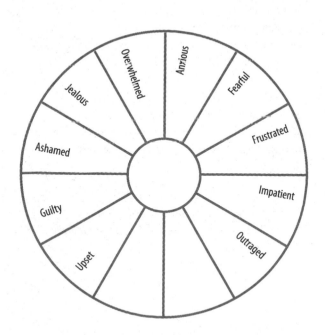

1. Bring to mind a difficult conversation with a particular person. Put a circle around any of the emotions in the diagram on page 237 that you experienced during the conversation. Add any other troublesome emotions in the spaces provided.

2. Which of these emotions do you find easier to manage? Put a tick next to these. Identify any coping strategies you use, such as starting to speak more slowly.

3. Which of these emotions do you find more difficult to manage? Put a cross next to these. Taking each emotion that has a cross next to it in turn, write down what triggers you to experience it. Be specific. For example:

   - "I feel frustrated when Alex refuses to talk."
   - "I feel anxious when Alex accuses me of going behind his back."
   - "I feel overwhelmed when Alex talks about taking early retirement."

4. Look back at the coping strategies you identified in Step 2. Which of your successful coping strategies could you apply to these harder-to-manage emotions? You might also find it helpful to think about using the following actions:

   - Taking a couple of deep breaths.
   - Suggesting a time out and going for a walk.
   - Noticing where in your body you are feeling the emotion.

Tune in

The purpose of this exercise is to help you to be more skilful at connecting with another person. You will identify which of the four "languages" of conversation you use most, so you can build on your strengths and also become more aware of the languages you tend to avoid. This exercise is particularly useful when you and other person are "talking different languages".

1. Bring to mind a specific person you want to have a conversation with. Read through the statements below. Put a tick next to either statement A or statement B, depending on which one most accurately reflects how you talk with this person.

A) Focus on what's logical. ☐

B) Appreciate what the other person says. ☐

A) Question and critique. ☐

B) Seek common ground. ☐

A) Use reason. ☐

B) Express feelings and warmth. ☐

A) Weigh up pros and cons. ☐

B) Look for points of agreement. ☐

A) Talk tough if need be. ☐

B) Make things pleasant. ☐

2. Keeping the same person in mind, now put a tick next to either statement C or D below. Choose the one that most accurately reflects how you talk with this person.

C) Focus on practicalities. ☐

D) Focus on the big picture. ☐

C) State facts and details. ☐

D) Use intuition and hunches. ☐

C) Use specific examples. ☐

D) Interact in an imaginative way. ☐

C) Consider the here and now. ☐

D) Consider future possibilities. ☐

C) Talk about what's tangible. ☐

D) Talk about what could be. ☐

3. Now count up how many ticks you have. Keeping in mind whether you are mostly As or Bs, and mostly Cs or Ds, read through the interpretations on pages 242–3. This table indicates which two of the four "languages" you are most likely to use and how to play to your strengths. It also highlights what else you might need to consider so that you can connect more fully with the other person.

A – Language of the Head	B – Language of the Heart
You connect with others through:	You connect with others through:
• Sharing your thinking and opinions • Finding meaning in what's said • Bringing together different ideas • Understanding the key issues	• Expressing your feelings • Providing a sense of warmth • Being willing to open up • Showing that you care about others
To connect more fully with another person, you may need to consider:	To connect more fully with another person, you may need to consider:
• Sharing how you're feeling, not what you think you're thinking • Identifying what's similar as well as what's different • Allowing others to express themselves even if it makes you feel uncomfortable	• Using your reasoning powers at times • Accepting that agreeing to disagree is sometimes a viable way forward • Challenging others when appropriate even if it means rocking the boat

C – Language of the Hands	D – Language of the Horizon
You connect with others through:	You connect with others through:
• Providing practical suggestions • Taking care of the details • Focusing on what will get done • Considering the *now*	• Using your imagination / intuition • Looking at the bigger picture • Considering future possibilities • Searching for patterns
To connect more fully with another person, you may need to consider:	To connect more fully with another person, you may need to consider:
• Letting go of your need for all the details • Allowing yourself and others to say "I don't know" • Talking about future possibilities even if they never happen	• Focusing on what's going on in the here and now • Dealing with the details of a discussion • Talking about tangible things that affect the current reality

Texture

The purpose of this exercise is to help you to generate a more dynamic, upbeat and buoyant conversation that sparks change. A positive texture *for a conversation comes from expressing appreciation, enthusiasm and curiosity, whereas contempt, disdain or disapproval narrow the possibility of having a life-changing conversation.*

1. Think about an important conversation you want to have with someone. Take a blank sheet of paper and at the top write, "Negative statements". Now, thinking about previous conversations you've had and following the format of the examples below, list all the things you *might* say to this person:

   - Showing disapproval – "I wish you'd listen to me!"
   - Being contemptuous – "You'll never be able to do that."
   - Expressing disdain – "I can't see why that matters."
   - Being cynical – "Nothing's ever going to change."
   - Being sarcastic – "That'll really make a difference."

2. Now take a fresh piece of paper. At the top write the heading, "Positive statements". Now list all the things you *could* say when you talk with this person, thinking about conversations you've had in the past and following the format of these examples:

- Showing approval – "I like your suggestion."
- Giving support –"I might be able to help you with that."
- Expressing appreciation – "I'm grateful for your help."
- Being enthusiastic – "That's a good idea."
- Communicating interest – "We could even go one step further."

3. Take another sheet of fresh paper. Draw two circles as shown. Make the circle for the positive statements around three times larger than the circle for the negative statements.

4. Review your negative statements. Look at what you could realistically say in your next conversation that is both grounded in the current reality and appropriate. Write these statements in the smaller circle. Aim to have no more than three negative statements.

5. Now review your positive statements. Look at what you could realistically say in your next conversation that is both genuine and appropriate. Write these statements in the larger circle. Aim to have three times as many positive statements as negative statements.

6. Commit some of these statements to memory. Have the intention to say the ones that are appropriate to the moment in your next conversation. Aim for a ratio of three or more positive statements for each negative statement.

Elephants

The purpose of this exercise is to help you to find a way of discussing what's currently undiscussable. Topics that become taboo, even though everyone knows they need talking about, are known as "elephants in the room". This exercise will help you to name these elephants and explore how you might approach talking about them.

1. Bring to mind a person that you are struggling to have an honest conversation with. Think about the conversations you've had to date and the different topics covered. Complete the table on page 248 by identifying topics as follows:

   - Topics that are comfortable to discuss (A)
   - Topics that are discussable but make you feel uncomfortable (B)
   - Topics that are undiscussable but would not actually make you feel uncomfortable (C)
   - Topics that are undiscussable and would also make you feel uncomfortable (D)

	Discussable topics	Undiscussable topics
Comfortable topics	A	C
Uncomfortable topics	B	D

2. Take a look at what you've written in Box B. What's made it possible for you to talk about things that make you uncomfortable? Think through:

- Values that help you to move through discomfort, such as fairness
- Conditions that are conducive to moving the dialogue forward, such as importance of the issue
- Personal qualities or resources you have drawn on, such as courage.

3. Now consider Box C. What makes these topics undiscussable even though you'd feel comfortable talking about them? Think through any factors you could change, such as finding a specified time to talk.

4. Review what you've written in Box D. Explore:

- What makes these topics undiscussable and uncomfortable?
- What would it take to move these topics from Box D to Box B?
- What advice would you give someone else facing this challenge?

Wheel

The purpose of this exercise is to help you to tell the truth to yourself about how you're feeling. Self-honesty paves the way for a Big Conversation. This exercise encourages you to be precise about what's going on inside you. Once you have this clarity, it is easier to communicate the truth of your feelings to someone else.

1. Bring to mind a conversation you're facing. Notice any thoughts or observations that pass through your mind about the situation. If you find them very absorbing or distracting, you may find it helpful to write them down.

2. Now close your eyes. Place your attention inside yourself. Take a couple of deep breaths. Ask yourself how you are feeling about the conversation you are contemplating. Allow whatever comes up just to be there. Notice any physical sensations in your body, such as a fluttering in your chest, a heaviness in the pit of your stomach or a tightening in your throat.

3. Looking at the wheel opposite, circle any of the words that resonate with how you feel inside. If a different word

reflects more accurately what is going on, write this down. Be as specific as you can. For example, if you feel "devastated", not just sad, then use this word instead.

4. Now pay attention to how this exercise has made you feel. What arises for you out of this self-honesty? If you feel a sense of relief or expansion, what does it tell you? If you feel a sense of foreboding or contraction, what does it tell you?

5. Finally, thank yourself for being willing to step into this place of self-honesty, self-awareness and self-acceptance.

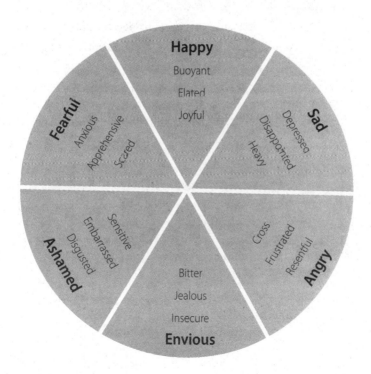

R.A.N.T.

*The purpose of this exercise is to help you to tell the truth to yourself about the other person. It invites you to express what you **Resent**, **Appreciate** and **Need** in relation to them. Once you have clarity about this, it will be easier for you to share your **Truth** with them when you have the Big Conversation.*

1. Bring to mind the person you are contemplating having your conversation with. Get in touch with any feelings of frustration, anger or resentment. Recall any specific incidents that have contributed to you feeling this way.

2. In the space provided in the table on page 254, complete the following sentence, "I resent you for …." Be specific about what the other person has said or done. Instead of writing, for example, "I resent you for always making me stay late", write, "I resent you for asking me to stay until 7pm for the third time this week."

3. Write as many statements as you can. Keep going until you feel a sense of release at getting some of these things "off your chest".

4. Now complete the sentence, "I appreciate you for ...."
Again, be specific about what the other person has said
or done: for example, "I appreciate you for trusting me
to handle the meeting with the new client last week."
Write as many genuine statements of appreciation as
you can.

5. To help you to complete the sentence, "I need you to
...", ask yourself what unmet needs are making you
feel resentful. For example, if you have an unmet need
for some recognition, you could write, "I need you to
acknowledge how hard I'm working by saying thank you
to me in person."

6. Look back over what you've written in response to all
three sentences. Put a tick next to any statements that
still feel true for you. You may find that some of the
statements no longer have the "ring of truth" about
them. Focusing on the statements that have a tick by
them, complete this final sentence, "My truth about this
situation is ...."

I resent you for ...	I appreciate you for ...	I need you to ...
....	....	....
....	....	....
....	....	....
....	....	....
....	....	....
....	....	....
....	....	....
....	....	....
....	....	....
....	....	....

My truth about this situation is ...

....

....

....

....

....

EXERCISE 16

....

Resources

The purpose of this exercise is to help you to identify the support you can draw on for a life-changing conversation. This includes the people, information sources and data that will make you more equipped to talk.

1. Using the diagram on page 256, list the specific resources that will help you to prepare for your conversation. Taking each of the three areas in turn, write down what's available for you to draw on. For example:

   - **People** – colleagues, friends, family, partner, counsellor, priest, neighbour
   - **Information sources** – grievance procedures, helplines, charities, websites
   - **Data** – emails and other correspondence, records, your notes

2. Identify any other resources you might also be able to get some support from. For example:

   - Mediation services
   - Support groups
   - Workshops (in assertiveness, for example)

3. Looking across the different resources, identify some specific actions that you can take. For example:

- Talk with my colleague
- Phone the helpline
- Book a place on the workshop

4. Finally, think through how you can support yourself and keep your energy up. Identify what you could do in the following areas to help you to stay strong:

- Eating well
- Getting a good night's sleep
- Having some time to relax

EXERCISE 17

....

Rewind

The purpose of this exercise is to help you to become more aware of your "inner dialogue", so that you are less likely to sabotage a future conversation and more able to think on your feet. An example of a completed Rewind exercise is given on pages 259–61. This exercise is inspired by the Left-Hand Column exercise in The Fifth Discipline Fieldbook *by Peter Senge, Art Kleiner, Charlotte Roberts, Richard Ross and Bryan Smith (1994).*

1. Recall a difficult conversation that left you feeling dissatisfied and/or had an unexpected outcome. For example, it could be when you:

   - Worked with a colleague
   - Received some criticism/negative feedback
   - Tried to discuss something with your partner.

2. Create a table with two columns. In the right-hand column, write out the conversation as best you can remember it. Use your imagination to fill in the gaps if needs be.

3. In the left-hand column, write out what you were thinking and feeling but did not say.

4. Look at the *feelings* you've written in the left-hand column. Underline the strongest feelings you experienced, making sure that these are real feelings rather than thoughts masquerading as feelings (the Wheel exercise on pages 250–51 will help you with this). Now consider:

   - When have you felt like this before?
   - What might the connection be between that occasion and this conversation?
   - Where else might this pattern appear in your life?

5. Look at the *thoughts* you've written in the left-hand column. Highlight any that show you getting defensive, blaming yourself or accusing the other. What impact did these thoughts have on the conversation?

6. Identify any of the positive thoughts that would have been helpful to bring into the conversation. Put an arrow next to these. How could you have voiced these thoughts? What are the actual words you could have used?

7. Looking back over this exercise, think about what you have learned about your inner dialogue. How does the voice inside help you? How does it hinder you? What can you do to make your inner dialogue have a positive impact on the way you talk with another person?

Teresa's Rewind exercise

Teresa is in a meeting with her boss, Jim, to review progress on fund-raising targets. Having reviewed the previous year, she presents him with her plan for rapid expansion of income generation over the next three years.

Thoughts and feelings not expressed	What was said
I'm feeling nervous about bringing up my proposal. →	Teresa: I think I can grow income by £3 million over the next three years. My analysis shows we'd need to recruit up to three people to be able to deliver this. Jim: (*Looks at watch, shuffles papers and screws up nose.*) Well, we'll have to see. I haven't got much time right now. So what's your solution? Teresa: I think we can stagger the recruitment of the three people over a three-year period … *Jim raises his eyebrows and looks away.*
I'm no good at speaking up for myself. (**Blaming herself**)	Teresa: (*Starting to stumble*) … rather than try to recruit them all straightaway.
He always belittles me and rubbishes what I say (**Accusing him**)	Jim: (*Sarcastically*) That will be interesting to see.
I need to set the scene here. →	Teresa: Well, I was thinking that there are some excellent people looking for jobs who've been made redundant recently. I believe they could focus on fundraising with the corporate sponsors … Jim: I thought that's what we had you for!

Thoughts and feelings not expressed	What was said
Why can't you appreciate that I'm already doing three people's jobs? (**Getting defensive**)	Teresa: I've already brought in £1million in my first year and, as I've told you before, I'm working crazy hours …
I've been consistently working 12 hours a day. No matter how hard I work it's never good enough for you. What more do you want from me?! (**Getting defensive**)	Jim: I know we've already had this conversation but we have different views about time and how to get the best out of a day
	Teresa: *Stumped, says nothing.*
	Jim: There are areas of weakness in your performance that I highlighted in your appraisal. You need to work on those first.
That's a separate conversation. I need to hold my ground. →	Teresa: I don't think …
	Jim: (*Interrupting*) I look forward to receiving your signed performance appraisal as agreed.
My stomach is doing somersaults. My brain is starting to go fuzzy. I'm really anxious.	Teresa: You know my position on the performance appraisal.
	Jim: We can discuss your plans once the appraisal is signed off. We can't have a sensible conversation 'til then.
	Teresa: These are robust plans, Jim. I believe they'd be really helpful in keeping this organization afloat during the recession.

Thoughts and feelings not expressed	What was said
	Jim: (*Looks at computer screen and then at watch.*) I've got to be getting on now.
I feel ashamed. I've brought this up at the wrong time and in the wrong way.	Teresa: *Stands there without saying anything.*
	Jim: As I've said, I've really got to be getting to my next appointment. You just need to sign off that performance appraisal before we have our next conversation.
I'm shaking. I feel completely deflated.	Teresa: *Leaves without saying anything.*

Table

The purpose of this exercise is to help you find a balance in conversation between getting down to business and building your relationship with the other person. When you are able to cover both, talking together can generate new possibilities.

1. Using the template opposite, on the left-hand leg of the table complete the sentence, "This conversation matters because …." Think through why talking together is important for:

    - You as an individual
    - The other person
    - Any other people on whom this conversation could impact.

2. On the right-hand leg, complete the sentence, "My part in this has been …." Think through how you have contributed to the need to talk. This might include:

    - Not having spoken out in the past
    - Being short-tempered
    - Not saying thank you.

3. Now turning to the top of the table, write down the topics you need to cover. Be clear about what you'd like to discuss. Be careful not to be too ambitious in what you want to cover in a single conversation. Prioritize topics so that you focus on what matters most.

4. When it comes to the conversation itself, put a firm foundation in place first. Say why the conversation matters and how you've played your part in the need for it. Once you've talked this through, then move on to cover the topics that need to be discussed.

WE NEED TO TALK ABOUT...

... childcare arrangements at the weekend including last minute changes.

... making the monthly payments towards the mortgage on time.

... the use of the shared living space, especially at weekends.

THIS CONVERSATION MATTERS BECAUSE ...	MY PART IN THIS HAS BEEN ...
... you're my brother and I want us to get on.	... not speaking out when things have annoyed me.
... the kids need a home at the weekends.	... being short tempered and self-righteous at times.
... keeping the family home is important for all of us.	... not appreciating how stressful it's been for you.

Afterword

I hope that reading this book helps you to cross the threshold into a conversation and a different – better – future. May the stories inspire you and the know-how enable you to make a difference in your corner of the world.

Having spent nearly a year writing this book, I am more committed than ever to helping people to converse at critical moments. My own experience has shown me, time and time again, that it is possible discuss even difficult topics without rupturing a relationship. When we find a way to talk about what matters most, we step into a larger version of ourselves and change our own life *and* the lives of those we touch. Conversation is how we evolve, both individually and collectively, as the body human living on this planet at this time.

A conversation is a humble tool that's available to every single one of us. Yet it can truly be a portal through which we can call forth a more magnificent reality. When we decide not to withdraw from each other but to turn toward one another, this one simple act makes a huge difference. It can heal a sadness, bring an end to an indignity and transform a tragedy. We do not have to live in the shadow of struggling to talk with one another. We can find a way to have *that* conversation, if we choose.

When we are no longer separated, we become capable of things we never thought possible. Come, let us talk together.

Sarah Rozenthuler,
August 2011, London

FURTHER READING

Blanton, B., *Radical Honesty: How to Transform Your Life by Telling the Truth*, Sparrowhawk Publications: Vermont, 2003

Bohm, D., *On Dialogue*, Routledge: London, 1996

Brown, J., *The World Café: Shaping Our Futures through Conversations that Matter*, Berrett-Koehler: San Francisco, 2005

Houston, J., *Jump Time: Living in the Future Tense,* Jeremy P. Tarcher: Los Angeles, 2001

Hycner, R., *Between Person and Person: Toward Dialogical Psychotherapy,* Gestalt Journal Press: Gouldsboro, 1993

Hycner, R. and Jacobs, L., *The Healing Relationship in Gestalt Psychotherapy: A Dialogic-Self Psychology*, Gestalt Journal Press: Gouldsboro, 1995

Isaacs, W., *Dialogue and the Art of Thinking Together: A Pioneering Approach to Communicating in Business and Life*, Bantam Doubleday Dell: New York, 1999

Kahane, A., *Power and Love: A Theory and Practice of Social Change,* Berrett-Koehler: San Francisco, 2010

Kahane, A., *Solving Tough Problems: An Open Way of Talking, Listening and Creating New Realities*, Berrett-Koehler: San Francisco, 2004

Kantor, D., *Reading the Room: The Four Levels of Leadership Dynamics*, Jossey-Bass: San Francisco, 2011

Katie, B., *Who Would You Be Without Your Story?*, Hay House: Carlsbad, 2008

Keyes, K., *Handbook to Higher Consciousness*, Eden Grove: Middlesex, 1975

Patterson, K., Grenny, J., McMillan, R. and Switzler, A., *Crucial Conversations: Tools for Talking When the Stakes are High*, McGraw-Hill: New York, 2002

Rosenberg, M., *Nonviolent Communication: A Language of Life*, Puddledancer Press: United States, 2003

Rowan, J., *The Transpersonal: Spirituality in Psychotherapy and Counselling*, Routledge: London, 2005

Schein, E., *Helping: How to Offer, Give and Receive Help*, Berrett-Koehler: San Francisco, 2009

Senge, P., Kleiner, A., Roberts, C., Ross, R. and Smith, B., *The Fifth Discipline Fieldbook: Strategies for Building a Learning Organization*, Nicholas Brealey: London, 1994

Senge, P., Scharmer, O., Jaworski, J. and Flowers, B., *Presence: Exploring Profound Change in People, Organisations and Society*, Nicholas Brealey: London, 2005

Shaw, P., *Changing Conversations in Organisations: A Complexity Approach to Change*, Routledge: London, 2002

Stone, D., Patton, B. and Heen, S., *Difficult Conversations: How to Discuss What Matters Most*, Penguin: London, 1999

Walsch, N.D., *Conversations with God: An Uncommon Dialogue*, Hodder and Stoughton: London, 1995

Walsch, N.D., *The New Revelations: A Conversation with God*, Hodder and Stoughton: London, 2003

Wheatley, M., *Turning to One Another: Simple Conversations to Restore Hope in the Future*, Berrett-Koehler: San Francisco, 2002

Zeldin, T., *Conversation*, Harvill: London, 1988

ACKNOWLEDGMENTS

Author acknowledgments

This book has been a true co-creation. Without the help of many individuals, it never would have been birthed. It's been nurtured by the care and kindness of the people named here and many others who are not named. My thanks in particular to those who allowed me to walk the path with them to their Big Conversation and for their permission to share what we learned together.

Deep gratitude to Neale Donald Walsch, not only for writing the foreword with such generosity, but also for changing my life for ever with his messages about the "new spirituality". His willingness to live his life as an open book has been truly inspiring. Neale's on-going support for my work since I completed his Life Education Programme in 2007 has made the world of difference to my confidence in running the A New You workshops and retreats for the spiritually curious.

My heartfelt thanks to Bill Isaacs, a true pioneer, for his creative genius and thought leadership in dialogue. Thank you to all the team at Dialogos in the USA and to my colleagues Cees Kramer and Andreas Priestland in the UK. I am indebted to all the facilitators and participants of the Leadership for Collective Intelligence programme and the Coming Into Your Own women's leadership programme for their good company and for so many creative conversations. I am also grateful to Cliff Barry for helping me to explore the deeper, darker contours of my personality through his exceptional Shadow Work®.

Thank you to Peter Garrett and Jane Ball, who have deepened my understanding of what it takes to talk when big walls have gone up between people, particularly through their extraordinary work with inmates and staff at maximum-security prisons.

David Kantor has been an outstanding guide in how to be a better interventionist in human-to-human interaction. Sarah Hill continues to inspire with her friendship and consulting work.

I extend my huge appreciation to the team of friends that formed effortlessly around the making of this manuscript. Tricia Grace-Norton accompanied me every step of the way: when I hit my wall, she held me; when I was in flow, she cheered me on. She gave me consistent, careful, clear-sighted feedback on each chapter over the 10 months it took to write the book. Tia Azulay shared with me her extraordinary gift with language and her expert editorial eye. Like an art teacher who adds a line to a life drawing that suddenly renders the image more accurate and more beautiful, Tia helped me to find my voice and to express it.

Conversations with Guillermo Rozenthuler – former husband and friend for ever – shaped the book significantly. Thank you for all the love we've shared and for him telling me his truth so I could get the book back on track when it needed it most.

John Higgins gifted me with insights that restructured whole sections of the book. With his help, some of the stories of my own life were coaxed out the shadows and I found the guts to write about them. Roger Cross riffed with me as I wrote, honed my ideas and pointed out times when I might cause embarrassment to myself and to others. Big thanks! My dear friend Karen Scholes helped me to sequence the seven shifts after we walked the chakra garden at Findhorn ecovillage in Scotland during a precious weekend away.

David Adams, a true elder, brought wise counsel on how conversation is strong medicine for the soul. Elina Koussis graciously edited some of the stories – and taught me a thing or two about English in the process. Phil Cartwright gave on-going encouragement and helped me to keep my eyes on the wider horizon when I got too buried in the book. Mike Wilson, a brilliant graphic designer, crafted the diagrams. Neil Anderson, a professor of psychology and of life, instructed me in how to stay sane while writing.

"Tonic talks" with other soulmates provided me with sustenance as I did my best to be creative on demand. Thelma Rowe, in particular, has been a real treasure. Ash Hansraj kept me company during what could have been a long and lonely winter at the laptop. My fellow spiritual travellers from the University of Surrey postgraduate course on Spiritual Development and Facilitation have also been great companions – Andrew Woodgate, Anita Hughes, Chris Frampton, Chrissie Astell, Peter Danby and Serena Atkinson.

My thanks to all the clients I've worked with in the corporate world over the last 12 years. I've been blessed to meet such accomplished people who've inspired me to keep on making a contribution in my own small way. I would never have learned about what it takes to have a Big Conversation without all the coaching and facilitation work that I've done. My special thanks to the British Psychological Society, who invited me to run workshops on dialogue for fellow psychologists and brought rigour to my practice.

Thank you to Adrian Moorhouse, Dominic Mahony and all the team at Lane4 consultancy. These Olympic medallists, elite performers and sports psychologists have all helped me to "up my game" in leadership development work. My thanks to Graham Lee and all colleagues at The Thinking Partnership for encouraging me to find my "edge" as a consultant and to deepen my own presence.

I am also grateful to each and every participant who has attended the A New You mind-body-spirit events that I've run since 2007. Helen Dunne and Brian Hill-Samuel, who hosts the Conversations with God discussion group in London, have been invaluable allies in helping me to launch my workshops and retreats. By sitting in the circle, talking and listening, I've come to appreciate how much healing comes when we share our stories.

Judith Seelig, a true yogi, has taught me about the body-as-communicator. Without her instruction, I would not have had the stature needed for some of my own Big Conversations. Sue Rickards, teacher of 5Rhythms® moving meditation practice, has led me to discover the joy of dance with no steps (and conversation with no script). Simon Cavicchia, my supervisor and master Gestalt practitioner, has kept me steady on my path as well as giving me a lived experience of true dialogue.

I did not look for this book; it came and found me. It was conceived in the mind of the commissioning editor, Sandra Rigby. I shall be for ever grateful for being asked to write the book I'd always wanted to write. What magic! Sandra's incisive feedback sculpted the book as I chipped away at the chapters. Fiona Robertson has done a fantastic job of editing the manuscript, providing challenge and support in perfect measure. Thank you to all the team at Watkins Publishing for their help with bringing this book into being.

Finally, enormous thanks to my family: Min and Dudley, Mum and Dad, Anna and Mark, Gemma and Ollie, Johnty, Emily and Tom. Our conversations have filled my life with love and my soul with laughter. May there be many more moments of joy – for all of us.

Publisher acknowledgments

The author and publisher would like to thank the following for permission to reproduce their copyright material:

page 96: from *Conversations with God: Book 1* by Neale Donald Walsch, published by Hodder and Stoughton, London. Copyright © 1995. By kind permission of Neale Donald Walsch.

page 107: Diagram reproduced by kind permission of David Kantor.

page 164: from *A Thousand Names for Joy* by Byron Katie, published by Harmony Books, New York. Copyright © 2007. By kind permission of Byron Katie.

page 188: from *He and I* by Gabrielle Bossis, published by Médiaspaul, Montréal. Copyright © 1988. By kind permission of Médiaspaul.